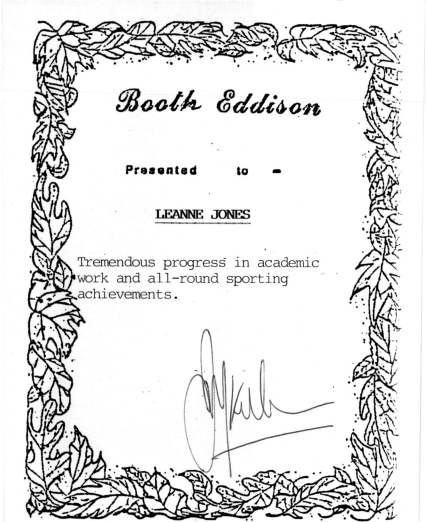

Booth Eddison

Presented   to   -

LEANNE JONES

Tremendous progress in academic
work and all-round sporting
achievements.

HORSE and HOUND
Book of
EVENTING

HORSE and HOUND
Book of
EVENTING

CAPTAIN MARK PHILLIPS

STANLEY PAUL

London

An imprint of Random House UK Ltd

20 Vauxhall Bridge Road, London SW1V 2SA

Random House Australia (Pty) Ltd
20 Alfred Street, Milsons Point, Sydney 2061

Random House New Zealand Limited
18 Poland Road, Glenfield, Auckland

Random House South Africa (Pty) Ltd
PO Box 337, Bergvlei 2012, South Africa

First published 1993

Copyright © Captain Mark Phillips 1993

The right of Captain Phillips to be identified as the
author of this work has been asserted by him in
accordance with the Copyright, Design and Patents
Act, 1988

Set in Plantin Light by SX Composing Ltd, Rayleigh, Essex

Printed and bound in Great Britain by Butler & Tanner Ltd,
Frome, Somerset

A catalogue record for this book is available from the British
Library

ISBN 0 09 174367 2

Photographic acknowledgement
The author and publishers would like to thank Kit Houghton for
supplying all the colour and black and white photographs in this
book.

CONTENTS

INTRODUCTION

Good horses are made. Some good horses get to the top without a lot of help from their riders and their training programme. More do not get there at all because although they have the ability to compete at top level, their riders have not produced them or trained them to maximize their potential and they do not make the grade.

That is one of the reasons why there are always so few riders performing at the top level. It is not because their horses are necessarily better than anyone else's. It is because they have the ability to make the best of the material they have.

The purpose of this book is to help the rider to maximize the potential of the horse rather than let that potential go to waste.

1

CHOOSING A HORSE

To be successful in horse trials a horse needs to be a reasonable athlete, a good mover and sufficiently supple and obedient to perform a dressage test to a respectable standard; in addition he must be bold and clever enough to go across country, yet careful enough to go clear round a show jumping course. Finding an animal with the temperament to cope with all three disciplines can be very difficult, for frequently a horse who is calm and obedient in the dressage lacks the necessary boldness across country and just as often a high-couraged horse does not settle in the dressage or mind hitting fences in the show jumping.

There is no doubt that of those horses who fail to make the top grades more are restricted by their mental inability to handle the sport than by any physical shortcomings. After all, the fences are not that big, nor is the dressage particularly difficult. It is the possession of the sort of temperament that enables a horse to be trained, and to use his ability in each of the three spheres, which is the most important factor.

The type of horse chosen will depend to some extent on what the rider is hoping to achieve. For one-day horse trials a half-bred or threequarter-bred horse will do and will be more likely to have the right temperament.

The majority of riders aspire only to the national one-day event and the one-star CCI, both of which put a greater emphasis on the standard of dressage because of the relatively easier cross-country. As a result people are tending to be attracted to the part-Thoroughbred and warmblood horses, who tend to be better at dressage and show jumping, and fast enough across country over the shorter distances. The Thoroughbred is often a more difficult horse to ride and train but when you get to the top level of the sport at Badminton and Burghley and to regional championships the Thoroughbred suddenly comes into his own because there you have got bigger fences and longer distances, where scope and stamina play a greater part and where the dressage does not always have quite the same influence.

Although the warmbloods are getting more Thoroughbred blood in them all the time, I personally would not choose one if I were looking for a potential international horse. My belief is that at the very top level of the sport, where horses have a 12- or 13-minute cross-country instead of the 10 or 11 minutes at the small three-day events, the Thoroughbred or seven-eighths Thoroughbred is the type of horse able to handle the extra distance the best. I would accept a seven-eighths-bred horse, particularly if the eighth had some pony, polo pony or stock horse in it, thereby adding an ingredient of toughness or wiriness. I have also ridden a lot of good horses where the last eighth has been an English hunter or Irish Draft.

When assessing a potential event horse I look for three things. First, he must be reasonably athletic, with a good sense of co-ordination and, above all, balance. A horse who lacks natural balance will be handicapped in all three disciplines and although he might get by in the dressage and show jumping he is going to find it particularly difficult at the end of the cross-country when he is getting tired. It is when a horse gets tired and when you encounter soft footing or unsuitable climatic conditions that all the inherent weaknesses seem to come to the surface. Second, he must have the temperament to cope with the different disciplines. Third, he must be sound enough to stand up to a sport that is much tougher physically than either show jumping or dressage.

Inevitably the search for such a horse usually ends in compromise. For example, my horse Distinctive does not have tremendous bone, and his cannon bones are quite long, but he is so naturally balanced and light on his feet that I felt these imperfections were unlikely to cause the problems they would have done if he had been heavy in his shoulder and on his forehand.

There is no doubt that first impressions have an enormous influence on the prospective purchaser. The initial assessment is best made with the horse stood up wearing nothing but a headcollar. If there is anything in a horse's conformation that worries me, it is the effects that those areas may have that I concentrate on most when trying him. Having said that, if when I ride him he gives a great feeling of athleticism and balance, I would be less worried about his conformation.

CONFORMATION

Feet and Legs

Sound, well put together limbs are vital in eventing, if they are to withstand the wear and tear of the sport. If there is weakness in the make-up of the limbs, then the strains of a three-day event are very likely to find it out. In the case of a one-day event horse it might be possible to get away with some shortcomings. However, the higher the level the horse competes at, the greater speed, the bigger drops and the all-too-often unsuitable ground tend to find any weaknesses. Anyone failing to take enough notice of the horse's undercarriage will, in ninety-nine cases out of a hundred, end up with problems. It is not worth spending three or four years taking a horse to the top level of the sport only to discover when you get there that the undercarriage is not strong enough to with-

stand the demands made upon it.

A horse's **feet** have to be good if they are to stand up to galloping on hard ground. Boxy, big or flat feet are prone to navicular, pedalostitis or side bones. I make a point of having the feet of all my purchases X-rayed, the cost being negligible compared with that involved in keeping and training a horse for two years or more only to discover that he is developing a chronic foot problem.

When viewed from the front the feet should be in line with the pasterns. I am particularly wary if they turn in (pigeon toes) and am careful in that case to look for wear in the form of windgalls on the outside of the joints. Feet which turn outwards, though not ideal, have caused me fewer problems.

The **pasterns** should be neither too upright nor too sloping. Upright pasterns do not give such a springy ride as slightly sloping ones and also lead to jarring of the horse's joints. Where they occur, take a close look at the horse's joints for any signs of wear (windgalls are generally considered a weakness but they are not serious in the older horse that has done a fair bit of work unless they occur in front of the suspensory ligament. I would not, though, want to see windgalls when looking at a younger horse). On the other hand, upright pasterns are definitely preferable to extremely sloping ones, because although the latter provide more shock absorbancy and therefore a more comfortable ride, they place more strain on the horse's vulnerable **tendons**. Eventing subjects the tendons to great strain and in any potential event horse it is important that they should be clean, cool and strong.

The horse should have good 'bone', with the cannon bones short, flat and of a good diameter. As I am just over 6ft, I have always looked for a 16.2hh or 16.3hh horse with about 9in of bone. Appearances can be deceptive, so I always measure the circumference below the knee by putting my top finger and thumb around it.

The **knees** of a horse who has been ridden should be free from lumps and bumps. If a horse has a lump on his knee, I would want a convincing explanation as to how he acquired it and would then watch his action carefully when he jumped a fence. A horse who is over at the knee is preferable to one who is behind at the knee. The first type of conformation is less likely to put strain on the tendons.

Viewed from the front, the **forelegs** should not be too close together, otherwise there is not enough 'heart room' so essential if the horse is to have powers of endurance. On the other hand, if the legs are too wide apart, he is likely to have heavy shoulders which can put a great deal of strain on the forelegs. Legs which, when viewed from the side, are attached to the front as opposed to the back of the shoulder give greater freedom of action.

'Tied in' **elbows** (i.e. elbows which are close to the belly) should be avoided because they restrict the horse's action, his leg technique over fences and his heart room.

As with the forelegs, it is important to search the **hindlegs** for signs of wear or lumps and bumps. Blemishes on the inside of the joints indicate that the horse hits himself when moving. The **hocks** should be big and clean, with no signs of thoroughpins or spavins. In my experience, a pair of curbs has never been a problem, but I would be nervous if there were

Distinctive has a slightly plain head which I quite like. He has a Roman nose, which you would not necessarily have from choice. It usually means that the horse has a lot of character. That is okay if it is working for you not so good if it is not. He also has a bit of white round the outside of his eye and that can sometimes place a question mark on how genuine a horse is. He has a good neck, a nice sloping shoulder. He is over at the knee, a bit long in the cannon bone and a little round in his joints. He has good feet. He lacks a little depth through the girth but has good quarters and a good hindleg, though it would be better if his hocks were a bit closer to the ground

only one. A lump which does not go round over the back of the tendon is likely to be a false curb, which is not at all serious.

Viewed from the side, the closer the **hock** is to the ground and the further it is from the 'jumping bump', the stronger the limb and the more ability the horse is likely to have. I try to avoid sickle hocks, preferring the opposite deficiency of a straight hind-leg. The latter would cause me little anxiety provided the second thigh was broad and muscular. However, a narrow and weak second thigh usually indicates that there are other things wrong with the hindleg.

Shoulder

A deep, sloping shoulder is particularly important in an event horse, being a good indication of his ability to gallop and jump. The neck should come out of the top of the shoulder. If it is positioned lower, the horse will tend to be on his forehand, which in turn puts more strain on the front legs. If the shoulder is

Get Smart has a quality head, a good eye and ears and a good shoulder. He is over at the knee, which is not a problem. He is a bit long in his cannon bones and a bit long and upright in his pasterns. He has good heart room, is short coupled and has a big jumping bump. He is a little weak over his quarters and a little short in his second thigh, but otherwise he has a well-shaped back leg

straight and the neck comes out of it rather low down, the horse is likely to find it difficult to balance himself.

Hindquarters

When assessing the hindquarters I like to stand behind the horse to make sure he is not narrow between the hips. For maximum power, long strong hindquarters are needed, not the narrow, short, rounded type. From the side, the jumping bump should be prominent but not so much so that there are no muscles around it. Such a deficiency indicates that the horse is not using, or has never been asked to use, the muscles in that area. In my experience, horses with the opposite type of conformation – the flat continental type of hindquarters – often find it difficult to gallop.

Body

Short-coupled horses tend to be stronger, easier to collect and better balanced than long-bodied ones,

Glenburnie has a lovely front leg and super heart room. He looks a little straight in his shoulder, though that could be because he is half asleep in this picture! He has a quality head and looks a little ewe-necked here, which I never mind because a ewe-necked horse always tends to be well balanced. He has a good shoulder. In this picture he looks a little weak behind the saddle

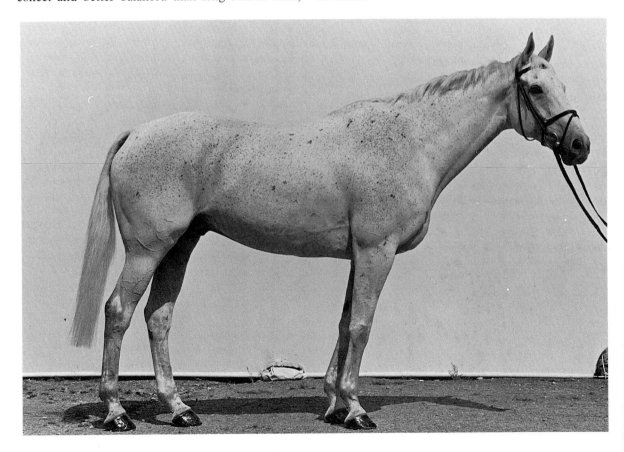

though I have had some top-class long-backed horses such as Columbus, Chicago and Lincoln. They found galloping easy and were great across country, particularly over big, straightforward fences. But the dressage and show jumping were more difficult because engaging their hindlegs to maintain their balance did not come so readily to them. If a horse is long in the back, it is important that he has a well set on or even slightly ewe neck to help him keep his balance.

The body should be deep, depth (like width) being an indication of the horse's power of endurance. But he must be in proportion. If a horse is 'heavy topped', it puts an unacceptable strain on his limbs.

Neck

Ideally the event horse's neck should have a slight convex curve, which will help with the dressage in particular. Nevertheless I have had some very good horses with ewe necks and they certainly need not be discarded provided they are good movers from the outset. They are usually well balanced, though it is more difficult for them to establish a good outline. A ewe-necked horse who does *not* move well should be avoided. Similarly a ewe-necked horse with a difficult mouth or difficult temperament is probably going to be too much of a problem in the dressage.

Head

I look for a Thoroughbred with a plain head, big eyes and big ears. I am nervous about horses who have a dished face as they are rarely brave enough or have the character to enjoy horse trials. I do not mind if there is a bump between the eyes, but I am wary about such a horse's temperament. He will tend to be more wilful, though if you can win him round to your way of thinking he will often prove the best at the end of the day. The important factor is to be aware of the risk you are taking where his temperament is concerned.

MOVEMENT

The horse's conformation can be assessed while he is standing still, but his action is also crucial and you should watch him being led in hand away from and towards you, at both walk and trot. I look for a straight, free, loose mover whose action is not too

close either in front or behind. I am wary of a pigeon-toed horse who turns his feet inwards, but more confident of one who dishes as long as the dishing is not excessive. The problem with a disher is that he is more liable to injure himself when galloping over rough terrain.

I am not too happy if the horse moves close in front. This defect is more acceptable behind provided the horse does not plait. Good shoeing, if necessary using threequarter or feathered shoes, can do much to help a horse who moves close behind, but very little can be done to help the more serious problem of moving wide.

Another thing to watch when the horse is moving is his tail. Clamping it in, or carrying it to one side, instead of holding it out in a natural manner, is indicative of problems in the back.

The **walk** is a good indicator of a horse's galloping potential. If he overtracks a long way he is likely to be able to gallop. If a horse is a really good walker, I would probably not even test him at the gallop. On the other hand, if he barely overtracks at all, I would ask to gallop him. Twisting a foot at the walk is another sign of weakness. It imposes extra wear on the joints and is often caused by a problem in the body of the horse.

The important factor at **trot** is that the horse tracks up naturally. I go for a nice round action but veer away from both the daisy-cutting show pony action and the exaggerated knee and hock movement of the Hackney.

THE RIDE

The important thing is to look for the athlete who is able to compensate for any structural deficiencies. The chief requirements in an event horse are natural balance; free, loose movement; natural spring off the ground when jumping a pole; a suitable temperament; and sound limbs. Therefore, if the horse is obviously an athlete, with a good temperament and tough limbs, minor structural defects can be accepted.

When riding the horse at **canter**, I assess whether he is naturally balanced – whether he has a long, flat, laboured stride and is very much on the forehand, or whether he has a naturally more springy type of action. You can both hear and see if a horse is naturally balanced because of the spring in his stride. He will not be looking for the same degree of support from the hand as the horse who lumbers forward on to his forehand.

At the **gallop** I look for a long, low stride. I would not choose a horse with a scratchy, quick, short stride. The good galloper gives the rider a great sensation of lowering himself to the ground. Although a young horse is unlikely to give more than a few such strides, all you need to know is that this ability is there and can be asked for in the months or years to come. It is often difficult to try a horse at the gallop because of his lack of maturity/fitness and/or lack of facilities. But as long as the horse has a good walk and overtracks well, then I would not worry too much about actually testing the gallop as in time he will learn how to gallop.

JUMPING

To test a horse's jumping ability it is not necessary to try him over large fences – the maximum in horse trials is only 3ft 11in. He must be reasonably careful but does not need the technique of the show jumper, who should bring his knees up so that the forearms are parallel to the ground. The event horse need not be so technically correct; he can dangle a little more, though not so much that he is likely to be careless in the show jumping phase. He should be an athlete, nimble on take off and light to land. As long as he has these assets, his jump can be flatter than that ideally required of the show jumper. Increasingly, a good jumping technique is becoming more important because of the technical demands being set both on the cross-country and in the show jumping.

I am wary of horses who are in a hurry to get back on the ground. It usually means that something is hurting them in their feet or shoulders and it always means that they do not enjoy jumping. The horse should give the impression of going up and out over his fences and he must relish his jumping, catching hold of his bit as he goes into the fence. He will only continue to be bold across country if he wants to do it. It is great to see a horse showing his enjoyment by bucking or shaking his head on landing.

You get far more idea of how genuine a horse is if you jump him over a fence in the middle of the school or the middle of a field. A jump set against the side of the school does not give a true assessment of the horse because it encourages him to jump higher than normal. Always try him over one in the middle of the arena.

You can always improve a horse's jump but I have found that the good jumpers are always good from day one because of their natural ability. If you have to manufacture too much of the jump, jumping will always be a worry.

MARE OR GELDING?

The majority of successful competition horses are geldings, because they tend to have an easier temperament and are therefore more trainable. Having said that, a good mare can be very, very good. I won Burghley on Maid Marion and was second on Gretna Green and third at Badminton on Favour, all of whom were mares. But if I were going to try a horse, I think my preference would be for a gelding rather than a mare.

HORSES FROM DIFFERENT BACKGROUNDS

Often the horse bought for horse trials is not a three- or four-year-old but one who has already done other things. As long as he is an athlete I am quite happy to take a horse on up to the age of nine.

Show jumping is the best upbringing for horse trials and it is relatively easy to find horses who have reached their ceiling in Grade B but who find the lower fences of horse trials, and especially the cross-country, more enjoyable. They will do well in the sport as long as they are not too common.

Ex-show jumpers can, however, pose various problems. They probably jump well but lack cross-country experience and need to be introduced to ditches, waters, drops and so on. Once they have been familiarized with such obstacles they rarely find them difficult. Dressage is usually the biggest problem, as the horses are often seven or eight years old and have to be taken back to the beginning to get them to look for the bit and search for the contact. It can take a considerable time because old habits are hard to eradicate. Re-education takes longer than education, although a more mature horse can be worked harder and longer than a youngster.

Racehorses provide another good source, but a

horse who has just come off the track will need a year or more of training before he is ready for his first horse trials. Most racehorses are unschooled on the flat and their style of jumping has to be changed. In racing they learn to jump long and flat; for horse trials they must be taught to approach fences more slowly, use themselves more and spend a greater amount of time in the air. Also they are unlikely to have been hunting and will not have seen water and ditches. Most racehorses, in fact, lead a rather sheltered life, and as a result their outlook is usually very naïve.

Good event horses are to be found in the hunting field, too, but I am suspicious of those who come from the show ring, because they have been made too fat and heavy topped. They rarely respect the rider and although they look flashy they can lack athleticism. Often they have been trained to produce eye-catching movement in front, but are not active behind. There are exceptions, but surprisingly few.

SUITABILITY

In both temperament and size, the horse must suit his future rider. He must be the right size: if he is too large, he may be too strong and be difficult to control; if he is too small, he could find it difficult to carry the weight. The other crucial factor is temperament. There is no point in the nervous rider buying a horse who is strong, pulls and has quick reactions. Equally, there is no point in a weak, ineffective rider buying a lazy horse. Horse and rider have to form a good partnership and the rider must feel comfortably in control.

It is best to take time over the decision and, if there is any doubt, to get a second opinion. Try to gather as much information as possible about the horse. Ask whether he has been hunted, jumped ditches, been through water, competed in hunter trials. If he has, ask people about his reaction; it will help you to assess his temperament. The more you know about him, the easier it is to draw up the equation of assets and defects. Try to find someone other than the vendor who has seen the horse in action and quiz that person about how he performed.

Looking back, I find that I have bought few good horses when I have been desperate to buy one. All my best ones have come on the market when my stable was full and I was not wanting to buy a horse at all. I only bought them because they were such athletes that I could not leave them behind. Never buy if your attitude is merely, 'He will do'.

THE VETERINARY EXAMINATION

If, after you have tried all these tests, the assets outweigh the defects and you really do want the horse, then the veterinary surgeon must be called in to examine him. I like to give the vet an indication of the problems as I see them, the areas which I am worried about, and ask for his professional opinion as to the likely effects of such defects as curbs, splints and blemishes. If I have noticed any signs of wind problems, I ask for an examination with an endoscope.

The vet should be made aware of just what is required of the horse – whether he is to be used for local riding club events or is being bought as a potential three-day event horse. A weakness might rule a horse out for the latter but not the former.

Very few horses receive an entirely clean bill of health from a vet and once again it is a question of considering the assets/defects equation. Assess whether his defects are likely to affect his soundness for your standard of horse trials and bear in mind that however talented the horse, he is no use to you standing lame in the stable. It would be better to buy one who is less able but tough enough to stay sound and therefore capable of withstanding the more consistent training and competitive experience needed for success.

It is becoming increasingly difficult to find vets who will give you an opinion because they are so worried about protecting themselves. A vet who says that a horse has such and such a defect but may go for 10 years and not be lame, or on the other hand could go lame next week, is no good to me. I am employing him to give an opinion and at the end of the day, when he has finished saying that the horse has this, that and the other wrong with him, the crunch question is: Does he think the horse will stand up to the work I am planning to do with him, and will the defects affect his performance?

2

TRAINING THE YOUNG HORSE

The training of the young horse should follow a logical progression. Always be looking and asking for improvement so that progress can be made little bit by little bit. The rider needs to be quick to pick up faults in the early stages so that they do not develop into bad habits. Better still, he should develop the ability to anticipate common problems – such as loss of balance, stiffening or a resistance – and take the appropriate measures to forestall them, prevention being better than cure.

To train any animal you must have an understanding of that animal. As a trainer you are instant judge and jury. You must always ask yourself, is the horse not doing what I want him to do because he does not understand what I am asking? Is it because he is finding it physically difficult to do what I am asking? Or is it because he is being bloody minded? In every instance if you make a correct diagnosis, then you will be helping to develop a partnership with your horse. If you make the wrong diagnosis, you will be taking a retrograde step because he is going to lose trust and confidence in you and often tension will be created between you which will take time to defuse.

The other basic principle of training is that little and often is better than one major grinding session a week. That way you keep the horse fresh and enthusiastic about life and avoid his feeling 'Oh no, here we go again' and switching off.

The training of an event horse is geared towards turning him into an all-round athlete. He needs to be the equivalent of a decathlete – a 'jack of all trades'.

To achieve this it is important to have clear aims and to understand exactly why you are taking specific actions. While there is continuing improvement, however small, I've always been happy. Often the difference between good riders and ordinary ones is that the good riders are always asking for the maximum improvement, but not asking so much as to create disobedience or tension, while the ordinary rider is frightened of asking too much.

Over the years I have found the following basic principles successful with my horses.

BACKING

My young horses are usually first ridden as three-year-olds before they become too strong or wild. The only reason I back them at three is that if they did turn out to be difficult, they would be even more difficult as four-year-olds when they were older, stronger and more set in their ways. Because three-year-olds are immature they should not be worked too much. As soon as they can carry a rider at walk, trot and canter (in the forward seat) and are steady enough to go for a short hack (in company at first), I turn them out in the fields to continue growing up and to get ready to face more serious training as four-year-olds.

I take a rather simplistic view of backing and do not spend hours lungeing or long-reining. I get on as soon as possible, preferably after about a week. The timing depends on the horse's character and tempe-

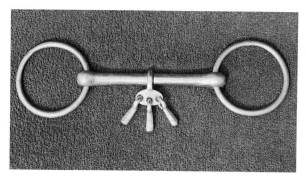

One of the first stages in backing is to fit a mouthing bit (above) and to leave the young horse wearing it in the stable for an hour or two each day
A Fulmer loose ring snaffle (below) replaces the mouthing bit when the horse has his first lessons on the lunge

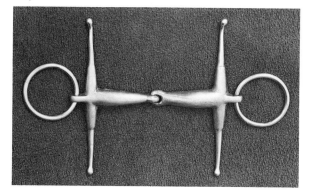

rament. If a horse becomes frightened when I start working with him, for instance when the girth is fitted or when the irons hang free during lungeing, it is essential to go back a few steps to give him time to regain his confidence and relax again.

Assuming that the young horse leads quite well, has learnt to tie up and have his feet picked out, the first stage is to fit a mouthing bit and to leave the horse in the stable for an hour or two each day wearing it. If his mouth moistens I repeat the process every day for about a week. If his mouth is dry, I might keep it up for a fortnight or more.

If all goes well, after two or three days of leading the horse about, handling him in the stable and putting on the mouthing bit, I start to lunge him, if possible in an enclosed arena. Where this is not available, a small area in a corner of a field will do. I use a Fulmer loose ring snaffle and for the first sessions do

The lunge-line fitted through the bit rings. Once the horse is under control the line should be attached to the cavesson

not use a cavesson but put a lunge-line through the ring of the bit and over the horse's poll, attaching it to the bit ring on the outside. This helps to give control in moments of stress, but is only a temporary measure. As soon as the horse is under reasonable control and understands what is required of him, I fit a cavesson. Using the rein unsympathetically while it is attached to the bit can damage the horse's mouth, so great care should be taken to avoid situations that may require a heavy hand.

To start a young horse on the lunge requires a different approach to lungeing a trained horse. With the horse standing still the trainer should walk back until he is level with the horse's hindlegs so that the whip can be pointed behind the legs. The horse should then be asked to walk on. If he does not respond, the voice should be used more emphatically and the horse should be tapped with the whip just above his hocks or on his hindquarters. If he walks on but then tries to stop, the trainer should keep close to the back legs so that the horse goes around him and cannot stop and look at him.

I keep the horse on quite a small circle and almost drive him in the beginning by keeping myself level with his hindquarters, taking care never to let the quarters get away from me by always following them. At first this might mean that the circle is not round, but it will become more regular as the horse accepts the situation. He will gradually begin to understand that he is required to move around me and can then be let out on to a larger and larger circle while I walk a smaller and smaller one until finally we adopt the classical triangular position.

The whip is a very important part of lungeing because it acts as the rider's legs. If the horse is rushing around, the trainer can keep the whip behind his back, but once the horse is settled, the whip can be pointed at the horse's hindquarters to encourage forward momentum as and when it is required. The lunge-line should be kept taut at all times. If the horse starts to fall in and the lunge-rein slackens, the whip can be pointed towards his head or shoulder, and if necessary waggled or flicked a little to keep the horse out on a true circle.

The other important early lesson is to teach the horse to stop. First, talk to him, saying 'woaah' or 'waalk'. Second, tug gently on the rein, and third, give a sharper pull on the lunge rein, always in conjunction with the voice. If he does not halt, move towards his head and if necessary direct him towards a wall or fence. Once he stops go out to him and reward him with your voice and a pat. Do not let him come in to you.

The voice is an important aid in lungeing. It is used in a high sharp tone to make the horse go forward and in a low tone to make him slow down. Its effect can be reinforced if used in conjunction with the whip (to go forward) or with the rein (to slow down).

The first lessons on the lunge for an untrained horse should be at the walk; trotting should only be started as his understanding, obedience and relaxation develop.

He can be lunged without side-reins for a few sessions, but I use them from an early stage, though not too tight. Once he is lungeing in a reasonable manner on both reins at the walk and trot, I fit a surcingle in the stable, with a breastplate or piece of string attached to stop it slipping back. This surcingle must be tightened very gradually and quietly, and the horse allowed to move about after each tightening. As soon as he is relaxed when wearing it he can be led out and lunged in it.

When the horse has learnt to walk, trot and stop on both reins on the lunge, side-reins can be introduced. I never attach them to the bit when leading a horse and only fit them very loosely when first lungeing in them, gradually tightening them over a series of sessions so that the horse is working towards a contact but without being behind the vertical.

When the horse goes forward wearing side-reins, replace the surcingle with a saddle. I like to do this in the indoor school rather than the stable because if the horse panics, he is less likely to damage the saddle in the greater space. Again, it is a sensible safety precaution to continue to use a breastplate or piece of string to stop the saddle slipping back. Also, when it is first put on it is best to remove the stirrups. The introduction of the saddle must be gradual and quiet. Ideally there should be one assistant to hold the horse's head and another to slide the saddle gently over the withers and into position. Again tighten the girth gradually and move the horse forward after each tightening. Then lunge the horse with the saddle on, first without side-reins then with them attached.

Once the horse lunges quietly wearing the saddle, the stirrups can be fitted. To begin with they should be rolled up firmly, but when he accepts their presence in a relaxed manner they can be let down to hang free. When he relaxes on the lunge with the stirrups flapping around, he should be ready for backing the following day.

Before the rider tries to get on, lunge the horse with the stirrups flapping to ensure that any excess energy and high spirits are used up. Once he is relaxed and calm, backing can begin.

I use an indoor school or similar enclosed space and have three people: one to hold the horse, one to give the leg up and one to get on. As with the introduction to lungeing, I attach the lunge-rein not to the cavesson but through the ring of the bit on the near side, over the poll and on to the ring on the other side. This helps the person holding the horse to keep control, especially if the horse rears up.

The rider is legged up to lie across the withers a number of times; when the horse relaxes he is walked around with the rider still lying across his withers. The rider pats the horse on the off side, down the neck and behind the saddle. If the horse is relaxed, allow the rider to return to the ground, then leg him up so that he slips his right leg over the hindquarters, taking care not to touch them. He should put his feet in the stirrups one at a time and keep his legs away from the sides of the horse. It is safer if a helper can guide the rider's foot into the stirrups to ensure that the horse's sides are not hit accidentally. The horse is then led forward and put on a small circle, as on the lunge, but with the additional helper at his head. Gradually the size of the circle is enlarged and the helper moves away from the horse's head towards the person holding the lunge-rein, and eventually out of the circle altogether.

The horse is kept on the lunge until the rider can control him at the walk. This might take just one session, but usually requires more.

During these proceedings it is important to use the voice all the time, in the same manner as in the early lunge lessons: at this stage it is the major aid for the horse, who will not understand much about the reins and legs. When starting to apply the legs, use nudges rather than unwieldy kicks.

When I feel reasonably safe in the school and can walk, trot and stop quite happily on both reins, I then take the young horse out for short hacks with another more experienced horse so that he gets some variety from schoolwork.

After being backed successfully the horse needs a holiday in the field, physically to mature further and mentally to digest the experience he has been through.

When bringing him back into work, probably as a four-year-old, in the interests of safety I would go through the same backing process again. Obviously second time around I find I can repeat the process in accelerated time, possibly two or three days.

EARLY RIDDEN WORK

Tack

All my young horses do their early ridden work in a loose-ring Fulmer snaffle bit, not an eggbutt. This is a mild bit which encourages them to take hold of it. In the initial stages the sidepieces help the steering – the bit cannot be pulled through the mouth in moments of stress – and they also help to keep the horse straight. It is important to use the leather loops to attach the bridle's cheekpieces to the bit's sidepieces, otherwise the latter will tip forward and the joint will hang low in the mouth, making it easy for the horse to learn to put his tongue over the bit.

I also begin with a cavesson noseband, but if the horse starts to open his mouth or cross his jaw I change to a flash or Grakle. I do not use a drop noseband because it is difficult to find one that fits and they tend to create resistance and tension in the mouth.

Normally the only time I use a running martingale is for hacking out a horse who throws his head in the air. It is also of value for jumping a horse who puts his head in the air and runs off at his fences. A running martingale should never be used for lungeing or for dressage because the angle at which it keeps the reins tends to make the bit work on the bars of the mouth rather than on the corners.

My young horses wear brushing boots on all four legs, prevention of knocks being better than cure.

Ideally, I would continue to work the young horse in a Fulmer loose-ring snaffle and cavesson noseband, without a martingale. But as soon as there is a problem I try to identify it and fit the piece of equipment to counter it. The actions of the various bits and nosebands are discussed in Chapter 12.

The First Month

The first month's work is aimed at getting the horse to think and go freely forward at the walk and trot on a loose rein. Roadwork will help harden his legs, but early work on the roads should always be done in the company of an older and quiet horse. As the horse gets fitter so this will help him to think forward more. The amounts of work and of food should be adjusted so that he feels well, enjoys life, thinks forward but is still controllable.

Very little work is done in the school: no more than five to ten minutes a day, and as much as possible of this on straight lines or very large circles. If too much is asked of the young horse, he might become bored and will not want to go freely forward. He will find small circles difficult, which will make him reluctant to go forward. It is better to school for a short time on the little and often principle, then hack out, preferably with another horse, both for safety and to give him more incentive to go freely forward.

At first he should only walk and trot, but as the trot becomes free and rhythmical then move on to short spells of canter. Make the transition into the canter on a turn or a large circle but then try to keep to straight lines and gentle curves, with the rider in the forward seat or at least with his weight out of the saddle so that the horse's back is not restricted by the rider's weight.

All this early work needs to be designed simply to get the horse to think forward and go freely forward from the leg in walk, trot and canter.

LUNGEING

The amount of lungeing needed depends on the character of the horse. In the early stages it is best to lunge him before the rider gets on and to continue with this policy if the horse is highly strung or fussy, or if he finds it difficult to keep his balance. If a horse goes well on the lunge, he need only go on it once or twice a week. The object of lungeing at this stage is to

Working on the lunge. Note the correctly fitted side-reins, rolled-up stirrups and protective boots, the tension on the lunge-line, the position of the whip and the author pivoting around a central spot

get the horse used to going forward into a contact with the side-reins without the rider on his back. Lungeing is thus used to introduce the next stage of the training.

Lungeing is also advisable for a horse who has had a few days off. When he is young and unestablished in his work he cannot be expected to start working immediately at the same level as before his rest. Lungeing can be used to re-establish that work.

Lungeing can help to establish that vital forward going attitude. As soon as you have some sort of control on the lunge you need to transfer the lunge line from the bit onto the front ring of a lunge cavesson. This will further encourage the horse to go forward.

The lunger must keep level with or behind the horse's hindquarters so that he drives him forward with the whip and makes him responsive to the aids to go forward. A similar approach can be used with a horse who is not tracking up, for such horses also need to be made to go more freely forward. (Make sure in such cases that the side-reins are not too tight.) At this stage the lunger will be walking the same circle as the horse, albeit on an inner track.

Lungeing with side-reins is a useful means of helping a horse to find his own balance and of enabling the trainer to see at what speed the horse is able to take longer, swinging strides. For this is one of the main objects of lungeing: to develop the horse's rhythm and cadence as much as possible without the interference of the rider's weight on the horse's back. The trainer can then aim for this speed when he is in the saddle (see page 42). The side-reins should be tight enough to establish a contact but not so tight that they draw the horse's head behind the vertical or prevent him from going forward.

The lunger should at this time be working to keep the lunge-rein taut so that it acts like the reins of the rider. If the horse tries to fall in, point the whip towards his shoulder and flick him out with it. If he stops going freely forward, move the whip towards his quarters and drive him on. When the horse takes the contact and neither tries to fall in nor stops going freely forward, the lunger should aim to pivot around on one spot so that the horse can work on a true circle. When the horse is on a true circle, with no sharp corners, it is easier for him to keep his balance, to develop rhythm and to take a contact with the side-reins.

If the horse tends to rush and take short, hurried strides, do not lunge him for more than five minutes at a time on either rein. Keep stopping him, changing the rein, using smaller circles and particularly constant use of the voice until he starts to relax and take slower, longer strides.

After a month spent mainly in lungeing and hacking out, the horse should be ready for more school-work. Most of my horses at this stage are worked for a maximum of fifteen to twenty minutes on the flat or over trotting poles before going out for a hack.

GOING FORWARD

The first aim in training a horse is to instil in him the desire to go forward and to get him to do so freely. He will need to be sufficiently fit physically and must be encouraged to *want* to go forward. It should not be necessary to kick and hit him to keep him going at whatever speed, and he should not stop whenever the rider's legs are still. If a horse is reluctant to go forward, avoid riding him on small circles. Try to work him in the company of another horse, in open spaces, in a variety of locations and as far as possible on straight lines.

In this first stage there is no need to work him to a contact; he may be ridden on a loose rein. The emphasis is on teaching him to respond to the leg aids at the walk and trot so that every time the leg is applied he immediately goes forward away from it. Until the horse goes freely forward from a light leg aid all training will be difficult and his competition potential limited to the lowest levels. The desire to go forward has to be achieved, free forward movement from a light leg aid being the prime requirement.

CONTACT

The next stage is to keep the horse going forward while asking him to work towards a soft, even contact with the hands through the reins. Initially there is no need to ask for any flexion of the neck. The rider must give the horse a light, elastic contact and encourage him to take hold of it. In order to do that the rider has to keep his hands still so as not to move the bit in the horse's mouth. This means that the hands should follow the movement of the horse's head whether it is lowered or raised. The same contact, with the same light, soft pressure, should be maintained and the weight of contact only increased for an application of the brakes or steering.

Many riders find this very difficult to do because they are not balanced enough and subsequently not relaxed enough in their arms and hands. To keep the same light pressure all the time the hand has to be very soft and the arm very elastic so as not to allow the horse to increase pressure in the hand or to 'drop' the hand.

The horse must also learn to step around the rider's leg. This will help prevent him from losing balance and leaning heavily on the hand. Some of this work can be done in the school but I am a great believer in doing serpentines and bending the horse around the inside leg while out hacking. At this stage of training the rider may need to carry a schooling whip or wear spurs so that he can reinforce the leg aids when necessary. As soon as the horse understands that he has to step away from the inside leg he can be ridden in a circle and with a more consistent contact.

BALANCE

Although later on it is important for the horse to find his own balance, in these early stages he should be encouraged to lean slightly on the hand. A slight lean on the hand encourages a horse to take hold of the hand and take a contact. It is a very common fault among riders to allow this lean to become too heavy. The horse then uses the hand like a fifth leg and does not learn to carry or use himself.

STRAIGHTNESS

Another aim in these early stages is straightness. The horse's hindlegs should follow the same tracks as his forelegs, on both straight lines and bends. If the horse is not straight, he will tend to lose his balance and lean on either the rider's hand or leg with his weight falling on to the inside or outside shoulder. It is therefore important not to have more bend in the neck than in the back. When going round corners, do not ask for more bend than is needed for you just to see the horse's inside eye.

The horse may well find it easier to bend on one side from birth. He needs to be straightened and then bent around the inside leg on his stiff side so that he takes an even weight of contact on both hands. Getting him to step around the inside leg, as discussed above, will help to soften the stiff side and assist the rider to control the hindquarters so that they do not step to the inside or outside of the forelegs. On the side to which the horse bends easily, the rider must concentrate on keeping him as straight as possible in order to get an even weight of contact. Too much bend to this side will result in the horse remaining heavy in the outside hand as he will continue to lose his balance through the outside shoulder.

SUPPLENESS

Suppleness is the product of all these factors. When working on them, it is important to train towards keeping and/or making the horse supple so that he is loose, relaxed and easily manoeuvrable. If he is not supple, it means that there is tension somewhere in his muscles and this will prevent him from working 'through', with no resistance. He will not swing through his back and his strides will tend to be short and quick.

During the first year or two of training going forward, taking a contact, straightness and suppleness are the primary aims.

INTRODUCING THE HORSE TO JUMPING

Young horses very quickly become bored with trotting round in circles and so I always try to introduce them to jumping at a very early stage. This puts variety and enjoyment into their work as most horses enjoy jumping and the variety helps to keep them interested in their work.

I start off by simply walking and then trotting over a pole on the ground. Once the horse is confident trotting backwards and forwards over that I add

Right above: An early lesson in jumping: the horse in trot stretches down over a line of trotting poles

Right below: The first stage in teaching a horse to jump on the lunge, with the poles set on a curve and the author walking level with the saddle

another pole 4ft 6in away. I am always prepared to adjust the distance between the poles to suit the horse because at this stage we want to make everything as easy and enjoyable as possible for him. As soon as he is relaxed and confident over two poles I add a third, and so on until the horse can trot comfortably down a line of six trotting poles.

After he has learned to trot over poles in a relaxed, rhythmical manner, I add a very low cross-pole placed 9ft beyond the last of the trotting poles. I normally just take away the fifth trotting pole and use it to make the sixth into the cross-pole. As the horse begins to jump the cross-pole more and more confidently, little by little I make it bigger. When he does this freely and easily, staying in a good rhythm I take all but the last trotting pole away, leaving just the one trotting pole, which is sometimes called a placing pole. However, the important thing is to use as many poles as are necessary to keep the horse in a good balance and rhythm in front of the fence. If there is any hint of the horse rushing or speeding up

coming to the fence, I immediately go back to using more poles – anything to stop any bad habits creeping in at this early stage.

This same process can also be done on the lunge (without side-reins or rider). Lungeing can be a good introduction to jumping as long as the horse is obedient on the lunge. The trotting poles should be on a curve and the 4ft 6in distance between them should be measured on the *inside*. When the cross-pole is added for lungeing, a guide pole must be used to prevent the lunge line catching on the wing.

If the horse does this exercise quietly on the lunge, it will often give the rider confidence to do the same

Below: Using the trotting poles on a larger circle

Right: Teaching the horse to jump on the lunge relieves him of any weight or interference on his back. Note the guide pole resting on the drum so that there is no chance of the lunge-line snagging on the fence

thing when on board. In fact there is something to be said for starting the process on the lunge when the horse is free from any weight or interference on his back.

When starting young horses I do most of my jumping out of the trot because at this two-time pace the horse has his feet on the ground twice as often as he does at canter, which makes it more likely for him to be able to take off from a comfortable position. When trotting into a fence I always use rising trot as this helps the horse to remain soft in his back and it is much easier for me to keep my balance. To be in the forward, light or jumping seat and doing a sitting trot is a contradiction in terms. A rising trot with the seat bones just touching the saddle every other stride allows me to stay still over the fence and make it as easy as possible for the horse to jump the fence (see Chapter 5, 'Jumping').

I canter at a fence only if the horse is relatively well balanced on the flat at the canter. I normally start a horse cantering over fences by adding fences after the cross-pole so that he takes a couple of canter strides before the second obstacle. If the horse is very free-going, I may put the fence one stride after the cross-pole but for the lazy or more immature horse two, three or four strides would be better because this gives the rider more time to keep the horse going forward.

OTHER TYPES OF FENCES

When out exercising I try to find little fences to trot over. If possible, I go with an older horse the first few times so that I can have a lead. I trot over gutters in the middle of grass verges, fallen trees or logs and small ditches and also walk through puddles, fords or streams. The more the young horse gets out and about away from the school and the more exercise he gets with another horse the better.

The emphasis should always be on small obstacles, so that the horse continues to enjoy his jumping and increases in confidence. The golden rule is: if in

doubt, do not jump it. If you are not certain about an obstacle, it is too big for the horse and it will only end in tears.

THE GOLDEN RULES OF JUMPING

There are the three Golden Rules of jumping: 1) the horse must be going forward; 2) the horse must be balanced; 3) the rider must wait for the fence and the stride to come.

These golden rules always apply, even at the very early stages of jumping. The young horse must be going forward into his fences. Often speed is the only way to generate this power and the desire to go forward. At the same time the horse will need help from the rider to keep himself balanced. The rider must therefore maintain a contact all the way to the fence and not fall into the trap of dropping the reins and shoving or pushing the horse at the fence. It is very serious for a young horse if he loses momentum or balance in front of a fence, for then he has an excuse to stop or he has to try very hard to clear it and might well not succeed. If he stops or lands on the fence, he could well frighten himself and lose confidence. Therefore the rider must go to extreme lengths to ensure that it does not happen. It takes five seconds of over-ambitious foolhardiness to frighten a horse. It can take five months, or even five years, to get that confidence back.

SINGLE FENCES

When starting to jump single fences out of canter, a placing pole can be used up to 12ft in front of a very small fence. The best distance for the placing pole will depend on the horse and should be adjusted to suit his stride. Later on, as the canter develops and becomes rounder and more balanced, so the placing pole can gradually be moved closer to the fence to encourage the horse to compress himself more in front of the fence. I have always found a canter placing pole in front of a fence very difficult to use and so tend always to start with a cross-pole out of trot and then canter a few strides to the next fence. However, some people use canter poles a lot and very successfully.

When the horse is jumping small fences well out of canter after a cross-pole he can be introduced to single fences. I like to have four or five scattered around the field. This makes jumping more varied and fun for the horse, and they can be jumped when it suits the rider and when the horse is going forward, balanced and in a nice rhythm. If I cannot achieve a nice rhythm, because of the temperament of the horse or whatever, I go back to trot or poles on the ground until the horse relaxes and then try again. Similarly, if I lose my rhythm through a loss of balance, I circle round and then try again.

If a problem does arise – if the horse stops, or starts to rush – it usually means that the rider has been in too much of a hurry: the fences have become too big too quickly or the horse was not relaxed enough. Go back to the trotting poles and gradually build up the size of the fences again. It is crucial in jumping to keep the horse's confidence. Always try to recognize when he is reaching his limits or starting to get tired or bored and, if nothing else, always stop jumping before he becomes frightened. Finish with a fence or fences which are easy for him so that he ends on a good, happy and confident note.

DOUBLES

A double or in and out is really only an extension of gridwork. A one-stride distance should not be tried until you are happy that the horse is going freely forward. I therefore often start off out of trot with a placing pole 9ft in front of a cross-pole, followed by 18ft (one stride) to another cross-pole. If this goes well, I take away the placing pole. As the fence is made bigger the horse will make more ground in the air so that the distance can be extended. When approaching out of canter, 36ft (two strides) then 24ft (one stride and the standard distance at shows) should be used, unless the horse is short-striding or the fence is very small, when you can start at 33ft (two strides) then 21ft (one stride) and lengthen the distance as the fence goes up.

Doubles must be built so that when they are introduced the horse finds them easy to jump. When he can jump through them in a relaxed, correct style they can be made higher and a spread can be introduced as the second element and then finally as the front element as well. The important point is to establish the horse's confidence by making them easy in the beginning.

3

THE DRESSAGE SEAT

When training a horse it is important to start with the basics: going forward on a contact, straightness and balance. Only after these basics have been established in the working paces is it possible to do more difficult work. The same principle applies to the rider. In his case the basics are the positions: the forward seat for jumping and cross-country and the dressage seat for schooling and dressage.

The aim is for the rider to remain still in the saddle, since any changes in the distribution of his weight inhibit the horse's action. Movement by the rider causes the horse to adjust by trying to move in order to come under where the rider places most of his weight. In the dressage seat the rider has all his weight on the seat bones with the feet resting on the stirrup irons; in the jumping, light or forward seat, the rider has all his weight on the feet with the seat bones having very light or no contact with the saddle.

THE POSITION

The classical dressage position is the one in which it is easiest for the rider to stay balanced and to keep his weight in the same position in the saddle. It is not a static position, for when the horse is moving the rider has to absorb the action of the horse's back under the saddle with his own back and hips. This is only possible if he is relaxed and supple, and it is only possible to be relaxed and supple if the rider is perfectly balanced. Any stiffening sets up a resistance against the movement of the horse, and when the horse

meets that resistance his movement will not be absorbed but will shift the rider. If he is unable to maintain his position, the rider will become tense and start to grip, causing more resistance and thus creating a vicious circle.

In the correct position the shoulder, hip and heel should be on a perpendicular line, with the weight equally divided between the two seat bones. Only in this position is it possible for the rider to be naturally balanced, just as if he were standing on the ground. As long as there is no tension to set up resistances, he can keep in balance with the horse and needs no support, either from the reins or by gripping with the legs.

The head must be kept upright. If the rider wants to look down, he should glance down with his eyes. If the head tips forward, it brings the body forward and the balanced position is lost.

The shoulders must not be rounded but should be kept back so that the rider's upper body is upright and straight. The back should be erect, neither slumped nor hollow, and positioned vertically above the seat bones, which bear equal amounts of weight.

The thighs should lie flat against the saddle and as near vertical as possible without lifting the seat bones. They must not grip the saddle as this leads to tension, which creates resistance against the movement of the horse.

The legs should hang down either side of the horse with the knees resting on the saddle and the lower legs kept quietly on the horse's sides. The legs should not grip. The hips, knees and ankles should be relaxed and free to flex with the horse's movement.

The balls of the feet should rest lightly on the stirrup irons, the body weight being directed into the heels so that they sink below the level of the toes. The stirrups should be of a length that enables the rider to reach them easily. If he has to grope for them, his heels will rise higher than his toes, and his body will tip forward. In this position the rider cannot be balanced and will have to hold himself in position by gripping.

The arms should hang by the rider's sides in a natural, relaxed way, with the elbows over the hip bones. The lower arm and rein are kept in a straight line and the hands held just above the withers. The wrists should have a slight tendency to turn the fingers inwards, the thumbs remaining on top. The elbows should not move from the rider's sides. The arms, wrists and fingers should be free of tension so that the rider can feel through his hands what the

horse is doing and when necessary move the bit in the horse's mouth without any movement of the arms.

All this has to be achieved ultimately without tension because only then will the rider's lower back and hips be relaxed enough to follow the horse's movement and to keep the seat bones in constant and even contact with the saddle. In mastering this position there is bound to be some stiffening when the rider has to make a great effort to keep his back straight or his elbows by his sides; but as the position becomes more natural, greater emphasis can be placed on relaxation.

THE WALK

The walk is the easiest pace at which to maintain the balanced dressage position because the movement is mostly on a horizontal plane and there is no moment

A good basic position

of suspension which tends to throw the rider out of the saddle. The rider should relax and follow the movement, follow the nod of the horse's head with the hands, allowing the seat bones to tip slightly and travel back and forth but without slipping to either side.

The sitting trot. The rider must relax and concentrate on keeping his seat bones in the saddle through having a rubbery tummy and lower back. Note the perfect line between shoulder, hip and heel and from the elbow, through the hand to the bit

THE TROT

Most riders find the sitting trot the most difficult pace at which to keep in balance. There is up-and-down as well as forward movement to be absorbed if the seat bones are to remain in constant and even contact with the saddle. Any stiffness in the horse's back will make the trot feel more bumpy and more difficult to sit to. Any tension in the rider will in turn make the horse tense against this resistance and go into a stiff, bumpy trot. The rider must relax and concentrate on keeping his seat bones in the saddle through having a rubbery tummy and lower back. The actual movement involves a slight rotation of the hips every stride in order to be able to absorb the vertical movement.

THE CANTER

Like the trot, the canter involves a lifting effect, with a moment of suspension every stride, but most riders find it easier to sit to since the lift is more gradual and not so sharply up and down and the rotation of the hips needed is more oval in shape. Again the rider needs that rubbery tummy and lower back to absorb the upward, forward and downward movement, and to ensure that the seat bones never move from the saddle. Many riders tend to rock the whole body back and forth but it is important if balance is to be retained to take the movement with the lower back and to keep the upper body still.

In all three paces the head and shoulders should stay still. If they tip forward in front of the balanced position on the perpendicular line through the hips and heels, the rider is forced to grip with the calves to prevent himself from falling forward. As he grips, the tension shifts his balance further forward, making him grip harder and setting up further tension.

The hips and lower back should absorb the horse's movement but the body above and the legs below should remain still.

TRAINING

Instruction is needed to acquire the necessary skills for all phases of horse trials, but it is particularly important for dressage. The best way of developing the correct position is on the lunge without stirrups. However, this method is only of real value if the lunger is experienced, has a good eye and is therefore able to help the rider establish his position, and if the horse is under control and able to work in a good rhythm.

Best use can be made of instructors not by using them as a crutch to lean on, so that they are doing all the thinking, but by listening to what has been said, understanding it and then going away and working on it. Anyone who wishes to ride well must work on what he needs to correct and improve and not rely on someone else. He has to think about the instructions, feel and work on them. Too many people have to be told the same thing two lessons running. There is only one person who looks at himself in the mirror and lives with himself every day on a horse. An instructor can give the information; the rider has to be his own trainer.

There is much to be learnt by riding, particularly if you are lucky enough to be able to find a schoolmaster who knows his work. Such a horse can be an excellent teacher of both dressage and jumping, enabling the rider to learn through feeling. It is also helpful to ride plenty of different horses to find out how to ride positively and not just be taken round the arena.

At canter the rider should absorb the horse's movement through the hips and lower back, keeping the body and legs still. Note the rider carrying his hands to try and balance the horse, who has become a little long

4

DRESSAGE

I have always believed that the three most important points to remember with dressage are to have the horse going freely forward from the leg aid; to keep him straight, that is so that you have no more bend in the neck than in the horse's body; and to keep the horse as balanced as possible for his stage of training. If you can remember these three things, while at all times encouraging the horse to seek the contact of the hand, your dressage training will at least be coming from a solid foundation.

TRAINING SESSIONS

The length of each training session will vary from horse to horse. The fizzy individual requires more work than the placid one because it will take longer for him to settle and for his mind to become receptive to schooling. The most important factor is to prevent the horse from becoming bored. If he does start to lose interest, he will cease to work and learn: he will do the bare minimum and he will stop going forward. If this does happen, he should be given two or three days off or do different work, but ideally he should never be allowed to reach that point. Training sessions should always be kept short enough to maintain the horse's interest and enthusiasm.

It is not just his mind which might become tired but also his muscles. When they have done enough and begin to ache he will start to resist. To avoid this happening, give the horse frequent breaks on a long rein and keep the sessions short. So often riders have their horses going well but then go on too long or ask too much so that eventually the horse starts to go less well and they have an argument.

With most of my horses, schooling on the flat is done little and often. After they have been warmed up so that they are going forward, are supple and listening to my aids, I work them hard for five to ten minutes. I am always very wary not to ask too much too soon, for if the rider asks for too much before the horse is settled or warmed up it always ends in a compromise, with the horse not going as well as he could have done. As long as the horse goes well, then that is enough and he can go off for a hack. If I do hit a problem, I might spend longer schooling until the horse is obedient (even if I don't manage to solve the problem), provided he is physically strong enough to take the work.

It is very easy to get so involved in a particular problem that time is forgotten, but it is better to stop frequently and to give the horse a walk on a long rein so that he can have a rest and the rider can think of possible solutions. I always ask myself: 'Why is the horse not doing what I want? Is it something I am doing? Does the horse understand what I want? Is he physically capable of doing what I am asking?'

At certain times it may be necessary to work hard to establish a particular movement. If you are approaching a breakthrough point, it is a mistake to give the horse a day off, because further time will then be needed to reach this point again. It is better to keep going until the breakthrough is achieved or for as long as you are continuing to make progress. Then you can reward him with a day off.

Changing a horse's place of schooling will help to prevent his becoming bored. But if you are on the verge of making that breakthrough, keep to the same place; in these circumstances accustoming him to new surroundings is a distraction and only wastes time.

Lazy horses are best worked as much as possible in straight lines or on large circles in order to keep them going forward. More forward going horses can be worked more on smaller circles. The size of the circles should be reduced gradually, but not to less than 20m in diameter for the young horse. Figures of eight and serpentines in trot can be used to make the horse more supple, loose and relaxed. These help a young horse to concentrate on listening to you instead of continually looking over the hedge at what is going on next door.

FORWARD TO A CONTACT

The primary requirement is to get the horse to go forward in a relaxed manner and, when he does so on a loose rein, to start working him towards going forward with a nice soft contact. In the first instance,

free forward movement may only come at the expense of the horse leaning on the bit and falling a little on the forehand. This is perfectly acceptable with the young horse, provided the weight of contact is not so heavy that the horse is no longer going freely forward and stopping himself up on the hand. Once the horse is going freely forward, seeking the hand and taking a contact, the rider can start to balance him and bring him up onto the bit by getting him to take a little more weight on his hindquarters and lightening the hand contact; but it is wrong to attempt balance and lightening before he is going forward seeking the hand because this will simply tend to bring him up off the contact instead of drawing towards it.

In the first stages of training the aim is to establish a feeling in the hands that the horse wants to take the bit down and away. If he just wants to lean on the bit and take the contact down as opposed to down and away, he will find it difficult to keep his balance, more weight will come on to his forehand and he will tend to take shorter, quicker strides. On the other hand, if he takes the bit upwards, either up and back or up and out, he will hollow his back, which will restrict his ability to engage his hindlegs.

Only if he takes the bit down and away will it be

The primary aim is to get the horse to go forward and to take the bit down and away. The rider has an excellent line from elbow to bit but is sitting way behind the movement in this relaxed moment, with the lower leg stuck too far forward

easy for him to remain in balance and to establish a rhythm in his work, with the muscles along his top line soft and unresistant. Ultimately, to test whether this has been achieved the rider opens his fingers and gradually releases the contact. The horse should then move his head and neck down and away smoothly, drawing the reins through the rider's hands, and not snatch or grab or wave his head.

To encourage the horse to take the bit down and away the rider must first work to maintain contact wherever the horse puts his head. The horse must learn that he cannot get away from the contact by drawing his neck up and back, or bringing his head on to his chest. The only time the weight of contact will be lightened is when he takes the bit down and away.

At the same time as maintaining contact the rider must keep the horse going forward by asking with the leg every stride so that he is pushing the horse over to his hand all the time, encouraging him to work towards the contact. He must also be conscious that any loss of relaxation, any resistances, make it more difficult to achieve this aim. This establishment of a light, constant contact, with the tendency to draw the bit down and out, is a gradual process. To achieve it the rider must work to improve the horse's balance, otherwise every time he turns a corner he will tend to grab the bit and fall forward on to it.

If the contact is not consistent, keep the hands still and every stride keep asking the horse with the legs to work to the hands. There is little point in asking for more straightness and subsequently balance until this contact is more established because without a contact to ride to it is difficult to develop anything.

The rider can test whether or not the horse is correctly looking for the contact and using the correct muscles by allowing the reins to slip through his fingers to see whether the horse wants to stretch his head down and away and to let go the muscles in his neck and back. This is an important part of my training. I use it during schooling sessions to rest and relax the horse and at the end to allow him to stretch his muscles and round his back. It is also important at the beginning of a training session as it tells you if the horse is warmed up, loosened up and sufficiently supple to look for the bit.

A horse can avoid seeking a soft contact by leaning or going above or behind the bit. When a horse is above the bit he raises his head and can then use his jaw and the muscles under his neck to set against the contact. To get him back looking for the bit the rider should use his fingers to move the bit gently in the horse's mouth, within the weight of contact but without pulling back and increasing the pressure. The movement of the bit in the horse's mouth makes it more difficult for the horse to catch hold of the bit. At the same time he must be ridden forward with the legs. Eventually he should drop his head. As soon as he does so the fingers should be kept still and the contact softened. This is his reward and eventually he will learn to associate dropping his head with greater comfort.

It is rare to achieve this immediately and permanently. Untrained horses tend to try to evade again and again, but if the rider never allows them to get away with it, and always applies the same corrections, in the end they will give up trying to resist. Such repetition is a basic principle in the training of all animals.

It is a serious mistake to try to correct a horse who puts his head in the air by forcing the hands down below the withers and attempting to pull down. This is not a solution. In this position the horse will find it easier to resist because the pressure tends to fall on the less tender bars of the mouth where he can set against the contact. He can also use the powerful muscles on the underside of his neck to resist against the hand. The other problem is that the rider tends to lose his balance, since by lowering his hands he is toppled forward. The solution is to hold the hands *higher*. It is then easier for the rider to bring the bit to bear on a soft part of the mouth, which gives the rider more feel and the horse more discomfort if he resists. As soon as the horse softens and relaxes, the rider's fingers are kept still and the hands lowered and softened.

The other main evasion is for the horse to curl his head and neck down and in, in order to drop the bit. Slackening the contact in the hope that the horse will bring his nose out is not the answer. The easing of the contact is exactly what the horse wants because his reason for drawing his head back to his chest is to escape the contact. Having achieved his aim he will therefore be content and will remain in the same position. If the horse uses this type of evasion to avoid taking the contact, the rider should follow the movement with his hands, keeping a soft but firm contact, and at the same time ride the horse forward with his legs and seat. The horse will soon discover that he cannot escape from the contact with the hand and that it is more comfortable, because the rider's hands are softer, if he accepts the hand with his head and neck forward rather than curled back. As soon as the rider feels that the horse would like to take the contact and stretch his head down and out, his hands should reward him by allowing him to do so. The principle is to make it easy and comfortable for the horse to work correctly but difficult and unpleasant not to do so.

Circles and figures of eight are useful figures for helping to make the horse more relaxed in his mouth as they help to get tension out of the system. If he is unsettled in his mouth, it might be because he is worried or tense and if he can be made more relaxed, the contact will become more consistent.

On the other hand he could have been badly broken, or something might be hurting him. Check to see if there are any possible causes of pain. Check his teeth and gums, the area around the girth for any signs of rubbing or pinching, and underneath the saddle for sores or bumps.

The bit may be uncomfortable, so check its fitting. If the horse rattles it around, use an eggbutt rather than a loose-ring snaffle, but as soon as he is quiet in the eggbutt return to the loose ring, because it gives the rider more feel and is a softer bit. If the horse does not want to take the contact, try a heavier, thicker snaffle, a rubber bit or a straight-bar vulcanite snaffle. If he has been badly broken or poorly ridden and is hard in the mouth, try a double-jointed snaffle. Again, as his mouth improves, return to the loose-ring snaffle.

The prerequisite of all this is that the rider must be sufficiently balanced to be able to keep his hands

The horse taking good swinging strides at the trot and seeking a nice contact with the hand, and the rider nicely balanced in rising trot

still. For if the hands are moving all the time so will the bit and then there is no way the horse will seek a contact. In fact, quite the opposite: the horse will drop the bit, giving the rider a light contact but in a false frame. Many riders shake the horse off the bit with their hands, think they have the horse light and balanced, only to get caught out when they try the more complicated movements because they have not got a true contact.

THE PACES

The Walk

The walk should always be on a long rein. The rider must concentrate on keeping the horse going forward by using both the driving aids and the hands, which should follow the horse's head movements so that they do not restrict. At walk the hands must move forwards and backwards with the nod of the horse's head in order to maintain a consistent contact. To make the horse take longer walk strides it is best to use the legs alternately. Apply the leg as the shoulder on the same side goes forward. This encourages the opposite hindleg, which is just lifting, to step further forward.

The Trot

The trot strides should be swinging, that is, not too fast and hurried or too slow and laboured, and the rider should try to establish a degree of balance and to keep the horse relatively straight. Balance, contact and straightness should develop together, but although the rider must be conscious of these aims, the most important one still remains to go freely forward. Without this, true balance, contact and straightness are impossible.

Going freely forward, with the rider in an excellent balance and encouraging the horse to stretch and take the contact down and away

The Canter

When the young horse is going freely forward into a soft contact at the trot he can be cantered on a big circle. It should be ridden in the forward or light seat and not for too long: 50 to 100 yards on one rein and the same on the other rein is sufficient at first. Over a number of days the horse will become more balanced and then the rider can gradually let his weight come more on to his seat bones.

In the canter, as with the trot, the rider must find the speed at which the horse finds it easiest to keep his balance and rhythm. This is often quite fast at first and to start with the contact in the hand can be quite heavy. It is important, though, gradually to ask for more engagement, shortening the stride a fraction and encouraging the shoulder to rise up a little bit more each stride. Thus the horse will start to become more balanced. As the horse begins to become more balanced, so the canter will become a little slower.

BALANCE

To establish a light, elastic contact the horse must first find his own rhythm at walk, trot and canter. In the early stages this means stopping him from hurrying or not pushing him too much on to the hand. The speed of the horse's rhythm should be such that in all his paces he should not be going so slowly that the work is laboured nor so fast that it is hurried. The rider must find a speed with a rhythm that suits the horse and in which he is most relaxed and comfortable and therefore best able to find his balance. This will vary from horse to horse.

The most common way for a horse to lose his balance is forward and downwards. The tendency is to lean on the contact and put his weight on to the shoulder, neck and head. This leaning on the contact is very different from taking the contact down and away, for then no additional weight falls on the shoulders, which are still light and free to move easily. The rider must distinguish between a horse who takes the contact down and out and one who takes it down to lean on: the latter is losing his

The Thoroughbred Glenburnie (Ian Stark), pictured here at Badminton: a typical example of a horse who did not settle to dressage until late in life

balance, and consequently he will be likely to lose his rhythm, quicken and/or shorten his strides. Even riders competing at quite a high level often find it difficult to differentiate between the types of contact. If the horse is heavy in the hand, ask yourself if it is coming from the mouth, later stiffness or whether the horse is simply leaning on the hand for more support and is therefore out of balance.

The way to change this misdirection of the balance is to engage the hindquarters, which helps bring up the shoulders and head. This is achieved through the half-halt (see below). Because each half-halt ends by lightening the rein contact it will also encourage the horse to carry himself.

The contact will only be consistent when the horse is balanced. Conversely, without that contact it is difficult for the horse to keep his balance and move with regular paces, because there is nothing for the rider to ride to with the legs and seat. This is why it is so important for a rider to develop a sense of balance so that his weight does not shift in the saddle and he is able to keep his hands still to establish a consistent contact. Riders who move their hands, thus preventing a consistent contact, may wonder why every time they try a transition the horse puts his head in the air, or why when they ask for lengthened strides the horse runs. By moving the hands they are often shaking the horse off the contact; he has nothing to take hold of to help keep himself balanced and they have nothing to which they can ride forward.

TRANSITIONS

Gradually the work should begin to include more transitions, with the rider taking care to see that they are done well. For the forward transitions move the bit to keep the horse's attention, at the same time applying the legs. In some cases, particularly when the horse is slightly underpowered and not going forward enough, it may be necessary to move the bit sufficiently to lower the horse's head so that he can still raise it a little in the transition without coming above the bit.

Riding Transitions

If the horse stiffens or resists in any transition the bit should be moved within the contact and not pulled back. The natural tendency when the horse takes hold of the bit is to pull back and not use the legs, but the rider must simply keep the contact soft by moving the bit and make it difficult for the horse to set against the contact. At the same time he must ride him forward, asking for the downward transition with the legs. Always ask for this to a containing hand; that way the transition comes through from behind and the horse is able to maintain his forwardness and balance.

It often pays, too, to do a number of transitions within a pace. Ask the horse to lengthen and shorten his stride a little in rising trot. Take care, however, only to ask for as much lengthening as can be achieved without causing the horse to lose his balance and start to run.

As the transitions improve, instead of taking ten to fifteen strides to change gear the horse should start to take only three or four. He should remain in balance, still with the rider asking with the legs and containing with the hands without pulling back. Accept that the transition may not be immediate: wait for it to come through smoothly.

Remember the different ways of using the leg aids. To go forward the leg aids are given in a series of gentle taps, and to slow down they are more supporting and less vigorous. The rider can support the leg aids by sitting a little more heavily, but the seat must be used carefully so that it does not result in the horse hollowing his back. The rider must also take care that his weight does not fall forward or back.

Transitions to and from Canter

In the early stages of training the strike-off into canter is practised on a corner or circle but as training progresses the horse should be able to do it along a straight line. It is a good test to ride across the middle of a field and to strike off one way, come back to trot and then strike off the other way and to continue striking off on alternate legs.

In the downward transitions take care that the horse is balanced and keep asking with the leg even if it takes 10 to 15 strides to happen. It is important to start with the same aids that will be used in the future, so increase the seat (but not so much that he hollows his back) and leg aids while containing with the hands. Containing the extra push in the hands should make the horse change down rather than go faster. If he resists, move the bit in his mouth with-

out pulling back.

As long as the horse is thinking forward, is balanced and is fluent in other transitions the rider can then try striking off into canter directly from walk. I usually start this in between the fences during jumping sessions. The forward seat takes the weight off the horse's back and he tends to be more forward thinking because of the jumps. This helps to develop the strike-off more naturally.

I ask for a little shoulder-in at the walk (see page 47), which puts the horse in the right position, and then apply the inside leg on the girth and the outside leg behind it and push my weight forward down through the knee towards the leading leg. At first there might be some resistance and/or trot strides, but the rider must keep feeling the way forward rather than jamming and trying to hold the horse's head down. His head can be lowered a little before asking for the transition so that the rider can allow a little more with the reins in the transition itself, thus helping the horse to go forward.

When he does the canter strike-off easily in the jumping sessions, progress to asking from the dressage seat, when the stirrups are longer and the weight is in the saddle. The important factor is to ride the horse forward into the canter. Avoid creating a struggle through tightening the legs and hands. Many people hang on to the reins and kick or squeeze in the transitions, which results in tension and loss of balance. If they vibrate the fingers and move the bit within the contact, then the horse will remain loose and supple and be able to step forward into the canter easily and without resistance.

These results are only produced gradually over a period of days or even weeks, as the horse learns to understand the aids better, becomes less tense and starts to use his hindlegs more so that he can go through the transitions with a better balance and less resistance.

In the transitions from canter to trot the rider must work to keep the horse balanced. On every stride he must ask with the legs, contain with the reins until the transition comes through from the leg. Initially this might take many strides, but this is normal and the aids should not be changed.

The Halt

In establishing the halt from the trot the young horse

must be given time. If he is allowed one or two walk strides, he will find it easier to keep his balance and to stop with his front feet parallel. It is difficult to establish a 'square' halt, with the two forelegs parallel to each other and the hindlegs also parallel to one another, before the hindlegs are more engaged and able to come more under the weight of the horse. The most important factor at this stage is that the horse does not step back, as this means the rider has been using too much hand and not enough leg.

The rider should accept just a short period of immobility when the horse can be patted and massaged by the withers which has a soothing effect. It is also advisable to talk and say 'Stand'. Event horses tend to be in a hurry to move off and not stand still.

When working on trot to halt, use the same aids as those for the earlier downward transitions, but make them stronger. In the first instance a few strides of walk are acceptable but gradually ask more positively with the legs and seat in order to reduce the number of walk strides. As they are reduced, the rider should start to feel the hindlegs moving in the transition to step up underneath the weight of the horse.

The halt: not the easiest of movements for the event horse, who tends to be keen to get off. Executed here with some aplomb. Note the squareness of the halt, the balance of the rider and the carriage of the left hand

If, in trying to establish the trot to halt transition, resistance is felt in the mouth or there is a loss of balance, work through by repeating the process, helping the horse to learn. Often if you try halting by going towards an unjumpable barrier or wall, it will help the horse understand what is required of him. Every time, soften the contact by moving the bit within the contact. Use the legs in time with the strides and do not tighten them.

Halt to trot transitions should also be practised. Move the bit just before asking with the legs in order to maintain the same frame. If the horse is given no warning, he can be caught by surprise and his head will come up. Again, I accept a little walk in the early stages, but gradually reduce the number of walk strides.

Simple Changes

Simple changes are often best introduced to the horse in a forward seat during jumping sessions but they must now be practised as they will be performed in the dressage arena – that is, the canter walk transition and then the walk canter transition on the opposite leg. It helps to work on them on a small circle because the horse is then more likely to remain in balance in the canter and to bring his inside hindleg underneath his weight. The rider must set up the horse for the downward transition to walk by keeping the leg on and increasing the weight in the seat while containing with the hands. If the horse snatches or leans on the bit, do not use brute force but keep the bit moving with the fingers, as in the other downward transitions.

Try to find a situation which will help the horse to do the movement. In the downward transition, head towards a wall. This will make him think more about stopping than if the transition is asked for while heading towards the exit from the school. Similarly, in the strike-off, try to find an open space to encourage the horse to think forward.

Horses are creatures of habit, a fact which can be used to help the training. When introducing the

The halt seen from the rear. The halt needs to be straight as seen here as well as square. The diamonds help the general impression, even if not at this particular juncture!

simple change, do it in a similar way and at a similar place in the early stages. This might make the horse begin to anticipate, but it does help him to understand. As the simple change becomes more established it can be asked for in different places and care can be taken to stop him anticipating.

Some horses do simple changes very easily but bigger, more backward ones might take a long time to come to terms with them. Make allowance for the different natural abilities of individuals and do not force a horse to do a movement. He will only be able to do it with ease when he has the muscles and impulsion needed to perform it and the correct mental attitude.

One of the hazards of competing is that it is all too easy to be precipitated into work for which the horse is not ready, which will only make him tense and resistant. If this is the case with the simple change, then accept two or three strides of trot and do not try to do it perfectly from day one.

THE HALF-HALT

Just as balance is the key to getting the horse to look for a consistent contact, so the half-halt is the key to establishing his balance. If the horse goes forward too freely and starts rushing, the rider should balance him not by pulling back with the hands but with half-halts until he can ask for every stride with the legs. The horse must not want to go faster than the rider requires.

Every time the horse wants to rush or speed up, the half-halt should be applied until he starts to wait for the rider. Speed must be controlled by the rider's leg and seat, not by pulling back with the hand, so that the horse is in the best possible balance and able to 'let go' of himself. If the rider tries to control the speed with his hands, he will restrict the horse's ability to take the bit down and away. He will also make him shorten his neck and hollow his back so that he cannot use his hindlegs so actively. Similarly, if the rider uses too much leg and hurries the horse, he will take a quicker, shorter stride and tend to lose his balance on to his head and again will not be able to use himself.

The rider must be able to use the legs for whatever purposes they might be needed – to bend around, engage the hindquarters or go faster. If the horse keeps rushing away from them, he will not be able to distinguish their different purposes and he will tend to hollow his back and become tense. If the horse rushes at trot, go back to walk, supple and relax him, then try the trot again and apply the half-halts.

To ask for a half-halt, apply the aids for a downward transition, maintaining the contact and restraining with the hands, but without pulling back, and with the seat and legs pushing the horse up to this contact. Keep applying the aid for the downward transition so the pace gets slower and slower. Wait for him to soften and relax as he finds his balance and the resistance softens and then, just before he changes down a gear, allow with the hands so that he can go forward again. Sometimes in the early stages a rider must ask for 20, 30, 40 or 50 strides before a horse will start to soften in the half-halt. Ultimately, though, the half-halt will come through in one or two strides.

The half-halt can be taught as soon as the horse is going freely forward. At first its effects will be limited, but as he becomes more balanced and sensitive to the aids so the effects will become more pronounced, with a greater transfer of weight on to the hindquarters. If the aids for the half-halt produce little effect, simply keep on re-applying them. It may be necessary to ask every stride for 20 or even 30 strides. It might take a long series of half-halts to achieve something which will be achieved first time with a more advanced horse.

IMPULSION

Impulsion is *contained forward momentum*. A horse who has impulsion finds it easier to establish cadence in his work. Cadence is a pronounced rhythm to the trot and canter. It is important to work on balance before impulsion. If the rider asks an unbalanced horse for more impulsion he will simply push him still further out of balance. Only when a horse can maintain his balance should he be asked for more impulsion.

Impulsion is a question of asking for more elevation in the strides in the trot and canter and of compressing the horse between the leg and hand. To create impulsion the rider asks with the legs and contains with the hands. If he pulls back with the hands, he will destroy the impulsion; he must merely contain the horse so that he does not go faster. If a horse is not balanced, this approach can result in a strong contact because the horse is being pushed out of balance. Once he is balanced the rider's actions will result in more elevation rather than stronger contact.

Getting the horse to find his balance and establish a soft contact are the keys to building up impulsion. The speed at which a horse can swing in his stride, let go of himself, find a rhythm and stay in balance must be found before impulsion is asked for. Thereafter it is a question of gradually building up the impulsion, with the rider never asking for more with the legs and seat than can be contained with the hands: in other words, never allowing the horse to lose his balance. If the horse wilfully sets against these demands for more impulsion, as opposed to losing his balance, then move the bit in his mouth and use more legs and seat so that he is pushed through the resistance. As soon as he gives, lighten the contact and keep the fingers still. If the horse hollows, then the rider is using too much seat and not enough leg. The seat must be lightened.

Impulsion is often confused with speed, in the same way that going forward is thought of as going faster rather than the desire to go forward. Impulsion is best thought of as elevation and is developed at the one speed at which the horse is best able to contain his balance and rhythm. That speed lies between the one when the horse is not going forward enough, and is lazy and not using himself, and the one when he is running and cannot find his balance. This speed is different for every horse; it also varies at different stages in the training. It is often easier to establish what it is on the lunge, because one can start by making the horse go too fast and then slow him down until the moment just before he becomes idle and does not track up. This is the moment when the horse should let go and swing through his back, and this is *his* correct speed. For some horses it will be faster than you expect. But for 90 per cent of eventers, whose Thoroughbred blood tends to make them onward bound, more often than not you have to slow the speed to give them enough time to swing and use themselves.

ON THE BIT

When the horse starts to look for the contact the first

step has been taken in getting him on the bit. When the horse looks for the contact *all the time* the rider has a contact to which he can ride. If he pushes the horse towards that contact with his legs, it brings the horse's hindlegs further under him and brings up the shoulders. This in turn will produce more impulsion, cadence, spring and elevation in the horse's steps. If the rider docs not have a contact to which to ride, the more he pushes the more the horse will quicken and run.

Many people think of 'on the bit' as a head position in which the horse's face is on or just in front of the vertical, with the poll the highest point. But it is much more than that. The horse must be going forward to the contact and he must be active, supple, balanced and responsive to the rider. Then once the rider can start to engage the hind legs more, increase the elevation of the stride and bring the horse's head up, improving the balance while the horse is still seeking the contact, then the horse is starting to go 'on the bit'. The important aids when trying to get a horse on the bit are the rider's legs. They must be kept on the horse, asking him every stride to go forward towards the contact, via the bit, to the hands.

As his balance improves, so the horse will stay more consistently on the bit. This is because with greater balance his hindlegs come under him more, his shoulders come up and he is able to carry himself better. In the early stages the trainer must be satisfied with the horse simply taking the bit down and away. He should work only gradually towards getting the horse to come up on to the bit, because he is only able to do so if all the other aims of straightness, suppleness, balance and so on are well established.

It is important that when the horse comes on to the bit he does not lift his head in resistance, but only as a result of the engagement of the quarters. Even when his head carriage is higher, the horse should still be searching for the contact down and out.

Once the horse is consistently on the bit the aids can be co-ordinated and will become much more effective. If the rider uses his seat and legs to push the horse forward to a restraining contact, the horse will change down a gear from canter to trot, or trot to walk, and so on. If he pushes with the seat and legs while allowing with the hands, it will result in lengthened strides, but if he pushes with the seat and legs and maintains the contact, the horse will go up a gear

– from walk to trot, trot to canter, and so on.

THE WALK

Many people ignore the walk, but it is a big mark earner in the dressage test. Practice of the walk movements – medium and free-rein walk for novice tests – does help to achieve better results. In the free-rein walk it is important for the horse to take long, free strides and, as the reins are released, to stretch his head forward and down. If his head remains high, it means that he is stiff in his back, and not seeking a contact. Then the rider has to go back to basics once more and push the horse over to the hand so that he starts to look for the contact again.

It is important for the rider always to keep the arms relaxed and to allow the hands to go with the nod of the head, only keeping a very light contact. If the horse is relaxed, he can be pushed towards the bit a little more, but the contact should not become strong and the rider should never pull back.

The transition between the free walk and the medium walk must be achieved on a very light contact. The horse has to learn that when the rider is gathering the reins he must neither tense up nor start to jog. With high-spirited horses this transition needs plenty of practice. It is often best done when out hacking, because unless you are careful the horse will anticipate in an arena.

When the horse comes back to the walk at the end of a session, it is important not simply to drop the reins, which is likely to make him fall on his forehand. Make him walk to a contact for a few strides; then let him stretch forward to take the reins, with the action, or propulsive force, coming from behind.

CIRCLES

As soon as the horse's balance and contact become consistent the size of the circles can be reduced. The approach to riding the circles must then change. On a young horse I ride a circle with the contact about the same on both reins. But using this approach on a smaller circle makes it more difficult to ensure that there is no more bend in the neck than in the body. Therefore the rider should gradually change to asking for the bend with the inside leg, which softens up the contact on the inside rein and controls the

balance and amount of bend with the outside rein. As the horse starts to turn, use the outside leg behind the girth in a supporting role to ensure that the hindquarters do not swing out.

It is no use trying to turn with the inside rein alone because the head and neck might come round but not the body. The outside shoulder will go straight on, falling out of line with the horse's body and leading him to lose his balance.

The horse must have reached the stage of looking for the contact of both hands before his bend can be controlled with the outside hand. Pushing the horse

The trot: Virginia Leng on Griffin in full flow at Badminton. Note the rider's excellent balance and the carriage of the hands. The picture is spoiled by a slight tilt of the head

with the inside leg to the outside rein lightens the horse on the inside rein, which leaves him only drawing towards the outside rein and enables the rider to use that rein to control the bend (i.e. easing the contact to achieve more bend). As with lengthening (see below), this will only work when the horse takes a *consistent* contact. If at any stage he avoids taking the contact, he will lose his balance. Consistent contact is the key.

The size of the circle can gradually be reduced from 20m to 15m or even 10m, but the same principle applies: if the horse loses his balance, then the rider must go back to easier work to re-establish balance, contact and straightness before starting to reduce the size of the circles again.

When schooling at home, and trying to do more difficult movements such as a tighter circle, if the horse begins to lose his balance, return to the earlier work, restore the balance and then try again. Try to feel when things are about to go wrong and stop asking for the difficult work *before* you 'lose it' and have to start again.

As the horse's balance improves the rider can ask for smaller and smaller circles. The smaller the circle, the harder work it becomes with the horse, therefore the more leg will be needed to maintain the impulsion and the balance. Ensure that there is no more bend in the neck than in the body: the smaller the circle the more difficult this becomes. If there is too much bend in the neck, the shoulder falls out and the horse loses his balance and his rhythm. The rider must work hard and needs quick reactions if he is to keep his horse balanced, in a good rhythm, soft, supple and with impulsion on a tight circle.

The shape of the circle is important, for by making the turns smooth and symmetrical it will be easier to keep the balance. I ride my circle so that there are four points to it. As soon as I reach one I start looking for the next. This helps to prevent any unbalancing sharp turns.

LENGTHENED STRIDES

The horse is ready to lengthen his strides when the basics of taking a consistent contact, going forward and being well balanced are established. With most horses I start working on the lengthening during the first year after backing. In the second year length-

ened strides should become more consistent and develop into a medium trot so that they can be produced when the rider wants them and not just when the horse feels like it.

Lengthened strides should result from the rider asking a little more with the legs and at the same time allowing a little with the hands so that the horse can stretch his outline a little, but not so much that he loses his balance and/or his strides become faster. Most people allow with the reins too much, which results in a loss of balance and the strides quickening, not lengthening.

Work on a circle can help in the development of these lengthened strides. On the circle, energy can be built up and the lengthening asked for as the horse comes out of it by the rider using his legs and asking more with the outside than the inside leg for a few strides, and then allowing with the hands.

With a young horse it is important to stop the lengthening before he loses his balance. If he only lengthens for two strides before he starts to run, increase the leg and/or seat aids and return to working trot. The transition should be ridden in the same way as all other transitions, that is by increasing the leg and containing and balancing with the hands.

Work on the principle that if the horse lengthens for three or four strides this week, he will give six or ten next week. Once the lengthening can be maintained for ten to twelve strides, the rider can start to push for a little bit more extension in the strides, always within the same balance and tempo but with a longer stride.

It takes time to build up the horse's ability to lengthen. In the first instance it might be necessary to accept a difference in speed in order to achieve some lengthening but this should not be allowed beyond the point where the horse starts to run, lose balance and shorten his strides.

MEDIUM TROT

Balance is a crucial factor in achieving medium trot, which is simply an extension of the lengthened strides. The rider has to ask for more extension but not so much that the horse is pushed out of balance. In training, whenever he starts to lose his balance, bring the horse back to working trot, reorganize and try again. The rider must think about the balance

every stride. At first the horse will tend to stiffen after a few strides. When the rider feels this about to happen he should bring him back to working trot and supple him up again.

Preparation is crucial to achieving the medium strides. The impulsion has to be built up and the horse established in a good balance. Then the rider can push with his legs and seat and allow with his hands to enable the horse to stretch a little. To help build up that impulsion I sometimes ask for shoulder-in (page 47), straighten up and go, or more often build the impulsion on a circle and then come off the circle at a tangent and ask for the medium pace.

The rider should make a conscious effort to let himself go. It is very easy to start gripping, to tense up and to bounce up and down, as opposed to pushing every stride with the seat and legs.

When developing the medium trot it is easier to

Virginia Leng and Griffin presenting a lovely outline in half-pass to the right

keep the horse balanced if it is practised on the long side of the arena or field and not across the diagonal. It is easier still if done uphill rather than on the flat. When attempting it downhill with a young horse it is very difficult to keep the balance and it should be avoided. Therefore always try to start developing medium trot either on the flat or uphill.

In the transition back to working trot it is important for the rider to keep the legs on so that the horse shortens up, with his hindlegs well under his weight. The transition is achieved through a series of half-halts from the legs, not by pulling back on the reins. This might take quite a number of strides, because the horse must not be allowed to become tense. As training progresses the transition can be achieved over fewer and fewer strides.

BEGINNING LATERAL WORK

I usually begin teaching my horses to go sideways away from the leg while out on hacks in their first year of training, but I wait until the following year before working on it in the school.

Ask for the first lateral work steps, in walk, along the side of a hedge or wall or the side of the school. After coming round the corner continue to turn the horse so that his head and neck come off the track. Bring the inside leg back to encourage the horse to step sideways, and rest the outside leg on his side to help him keep his balance. The outside rein supports the horse and stops him going further forward in the turn. The inside rein is used to keep a soft contact and to establish a slight bend.

As the horse begins to understand what is required of him and goes sideways with increasing ease, apply the inside leg further and further forward until it is close to the girth. This helps to establish a bend and makes it easier to keep the inside rein soft. It will also help to turn this sideways movement from the easier leg-yielding into shoulder-in.

It is important to keep up the same rhythm whether going in straight lines or sideways. The shallower the angle of the lateral work, the easier it is for the horse to maintain forwardness, so initially only turn a little off the track. As he understands and relaxes, gradually increase the angle. I always start in walk and then progress to asking for the same things in trot and canter.

SHOULDER-IN

Shoulder-in at walk and trot is the exercise I use more than any other to help keep a horse supple, to encourage him to use his inside hindleg more actively and to help straighten him. When the horse is going correctly in shoulder-in he should be on three tracks.

Shoulder-in, a useful exercise to get a horse supple. The shoulder-in should be on three tracks, as shown here, though the rider seems to be pushing the quarters out rather than bringing the shoulder in

As the horse progresses the rider must work more towards getting him to take the outside rein and to keep only a light contact on the inside one. Many riders tighten up in this movement, particularly in trot, and tend to pull the inside leg back. They stiffen up and cannot then follow the horse's movements. It is very easy to let one or the other hand drop down below the withers and become fixed instead of carrying a pair of hands above the withers all the time.

As he turns the horse's shoulders off the track, the rider must turn his own shoulders so that they stay in alignment with those of the horse, while the hip bones stay parallel to the horse's hips and at 90 per cent to the track. The rider must also remain just as relaxed and soft with his hands as when he was going straight forward. The seat can be used to keep up the same rhythm as was established before going into the shoulder-in.

HALF-PASS

Training for the half-pass should be started in walk, which makes it easier to keep the balance and gives the rider time to think what to do and apply the correct aids. I usually wear spurs and carry a whip to give me extra aids until the horse understands what he should be doing.

I always start with shoulder-in so that I have the correct bend and the horse set correctly and then switch to asking for the half-pass, always towards an open space to encourage the horse to keep going forward. Keep the bend without pulling back with the inside hand. If too much inside hand is used, it stops the horse from going forward. Keep moving the fingers on this inside rein but do not pull back. At the same time allow enough with the outside hand so that he can bend to the inside, and keep the inside leg on the girth to keep him going forward. The outside leg taps the horse behind the girth to get his hindlegs to cross over, and this leg should not tighten; it is far more effective if it taps or kicks every stride. I also try and keep my weight slightly to the side of the direction I'm going to encourage the horse to go that way. In any event the weight must not come out.

Each of the rider's hands and legs has to do something different. It is easy to become tense and tight and not to keep the hips moving with the horse. Most of my concentration goes into keeping myself soft

and relaxed and not tightening against the horse. If he resists, it is even easier to tighten against him.

It is easiest for the rider to stay relaxed at the walk. Often I will then try at the canter and finally at the trot. It is easier to keep balanced in canter than trot.

Any difficulties in getting the bend are a result of tension in the rider or the horse, or both. If both remain relaxed, there is no reason why the bend cannot be maintained. As soon as there is resistance and the bend is lost, the strides will get shorter and shorter

Left: At half-pass each of the rider's hands and legs has to do something different. A good half-pass, although the rider should not be crossing his left hand over the withers and he should have a little more weight on his left seat bone

Right: Counter-canter. Note that there is not quite enough bend over the leading leg but the rider is carrying an excellent pair of hands

and the half-pass become more of a struggle.

Riders often tighten, pulling on the inside rein instead of asking and giving. The rider should be thinking all the time of giving, allowing the horse to stretch and seek the contact in the direction of the half-pass, so that he draws himself to the direction he is going.

COUNTER-CANTER

As the horse becomes more balanced in the canter, the counter-canter can be asked for in deeper and deeper loops. If at any time the horse loses his balance, ask for a shallower loop the next time. The rider must concentrate on maintaining the bend towards the leading leg and keeping the horse balanced.

The rider's leg on the side of the horse's leading

leg and to which the horse is bent should be kept on the girth and used to keep up the impulsion and to help maintain the bend. The other leg is applied behind the girth and used quite strongly if the quarters start to swing in on the circle.

Initially with a young horse the problem is to keep him balanced and to prevent him leaning on the hand. If you start with big enough loops, though, it should be quite easy to maintain the balance, the bend and the counter-canter. As the canter improves so the balance improves and you can start to ask for a tighter and tighter circle.

MEDIUM CANTER

The medium canter should be worked on in a similar way to the medium trot. It is easier to work on this movement in a field, where the extra space makes it easier to keep a consistent balance. When the horse is reasonably proficient in the field he can be tried in an arena.

Start by developing a little going and coming. Try to get the horse to lengthen his frame and strides, and to lower himself without increasing the revs. He should be drawing towards the bit so that when the rider allows slightly with the reins he will stretch and lower his head and neck but still keep his shoulders coming up. He should develop the medium strides by pushing from behind and not by pulling himself along with his front legs. To achieve this, ask with the legs before allowing with the hands and do not lean forward. Ask with the legs every stride just before the shoulders come up. If the horse starts to quicken, the rider has asked too much, and the horse has lost his balance or he is not seeking a genuine contact and is therefore quickening instead of seeking the contact, stretching and lengthening.

REIN-BACK

The way in which I teach this movement depends on the type of horse. If he is onward bound, I tend to do

The 10m circle at canter. It is always difficult not to lose the shoulder and to keep the horse balanced in this movement

a number of rein-backs during his jumping training. I stop him, rein back, and strike off again and repeat the exercise a number of times. For the forward going horse it helps to keep him balanced and get him to wait for the leg aid, and for the idle horse it is an excellent exercise to get his hocks more under his weight and to make him more responsive to coming and going.

My normal aids for the rein-back are to lighten the weight on my seat bones, move the bit in the horse's mouth and ask with my legs. If he does not understand, then I ask someone to stand in front and tap him on the knees at the same time as I give the aids. The rider should not pull back with the reins because the horse will simply resist.

Another aid to the rein-back is derived from the tendency of most horses to move the same leg first. To begin with I ask with my leg on that same side. This helps the horse to go back straight and not to swing his quarters.

If the horse does not go back straight, the rein-back should be practised alongside a hedge or wall, which will prevent the quarters veering to that side.

TRAINING PROBLEMS

Use of Psychology
Psychology is vital when tackling problems during training. I have learnt to think like a horse. If a horse is not responding to my aids, I ask myself: Is he feeling so well that he has excessive high spirits? Does he understand? Is he finding it difficult to do what is requested? Is he being asked to do too much for the stage of his training? Is he being obstinate or lazy? Is he bored, under-exercised or tired?

Whenever there is a problem and something is not being achieved it is essential to find out the reason. You must keep asking, 'Why?'

Use of Relaxation
When the horse resists, the tendency is for the rider to fight back, which leads to both horse and rider tightening and becoming more tense. The rider must stay loose and supple, otherwise his tension sets up further resistances from the horse. The horse can only resist if the rider gives him something to resist against.

This is something I wrestle with all the time. If the

rider is relaxed, particularly in his seat, arms and hands, it encourages the horse to relax and his tension is thus unwound and dispelled. When the rider is relaxed it is also easier to correct resistance within a movement, which is preferable to returning to suppling exercises to re-establish softness. The more tense the horse, the more the rider must relax, and the rider must relax before you can expect the horse to relax. It is easy to say but very difficult to do, which is why the rider has to continuously make a conscious effort to stay relaxed and soft all the time.

Lack of Attention

A horse can use any excuse to spook, put his head in the air and not work, especially event horses as they become fitter.

Wherever possible take the horse away from the thing that is distracting him. Either the horse is going to be taught to trot past paper, or he is going to be taught a movement, but he cannot be taught both at the same time. Keep your hands high, keep the contact and ride him forward until he relaxes enough to accept both the hands and the legs. The rider should always keep the aid there albeit softly but firmly until the horse starts to accept there is no escape. Keep the rhythm very slow to help maintain control and to prevent the horse from rushing away from the aids. With some horses it might be better to return to walk and maybe do some lateral work before returning to trot.

Inattentiveness is infuriating for the rider, who can all too easily become impatient. This is not the answer, so if you are in danger of losing patience, it is best to get off and try lungeing. An angry rider simply makes the horse more tense.

Try to prevent the problem arising in the first place. If a horse has been under-exercised, is a bit stiff or is highly strung, hack him out before starting to school. The lazy horse, on the other hand, is usually easier to train after a rest.

Running On

Most event horses want to go faster than required. They have to be much fitter than horses in other disciplines, and this makes them even keener. To solve this problem, stay in rising trot and use half-halts until the horse lets go of himself and starts to swing. Then he can be ridden forward with the leg. Work on circles, figures of eight and serpentines rather than straight lines. If time permits at a competition, and certainly at home, I often ride, lunge, ride, lunge until I can ride the horse forward with the leg instead of restraining him with the hand.

Stiffness

The horse should not be stiff but should let go of his muscles, particularly through his back and neck. To achieve this, use rising trot and keep turning. In canter use the forward or a very light seat. After cantering try leg-yielding in trot. Other good exercises to release stiffness are shoulder-in, quarters-in and half-pass. I'm a great believer in first of all getting rid of any lateral stiffness in walk and then progressing to achieving the same thing in trot and canter. Often, though, this perceived stiffness or heaviness is caused by the rider allowing the horse to lean on one hand or the other.

Because an event horse needs to be high-couraged to jump across country he tends to find it difficult to let go of himself and rid himself of tension. This in turn makes it difficult for the rider to keep him supple. Even after being worked along the lines suggested above, he will often tighten up again when asked to perform certain movements.

The rider must react immediately to reduce the tension and keep the horse soft. Initially try to do this within the movement; failing that, take him back to leg-yielding or, if the tightness is in his neck, soften the contact and bend him to the side on which he is hard and tense. Take care to work for this softness with both the hand and the leg. If the hand alone is used, the horse tends to set against it and resist.

If the tension is due to physical problems or to the horse being worried, then make allowances and do not ask too much. The important thing is to keep him relaxed and rideable, and to achieve this it helps, as explained above, if the rider stays supple and relaxed.

Again, the important factor is to work out why he is stiff. Is he worried? Is he setting himself against the contact? Does he lack balance? Is he inattentive?

Stiffness and tension are constant problems. A great deal of the skill of riding is anticipating a build-up of tension or a loss of balance before it happens. The problem is best prevented before it occurs. If the rider is slow to react, then the problem becomes more established and needs a bigger correction.

Resisting in Transitions

The same principles apply through all the transitions. If there is a problem, balance is crucial and must be maintained or restored through half-halts, with the rider asking for more engagement. At the same time the contact must be kept soft by moving the bit within that contact.

The two transitions that create most problems are the canter strike-off and the halt.

If the rider is anxious that the horse might come above the bit in the strike-off, the worst thing he can do is to take a stronger contact with the hands before asking for the transition. This makes the problem worse because it gives the horse something to set

Extended trot, with the rider using a lot of seat

against. With too much hand and not enough leg the horse loses impulsion and his head comes up. Instead, ride forward positively by using more inside leg and keep the horse soft by vibrating the fingers and making it more difficult for him to set against the hands. Keeping the horse soft is vital and the rider will find it helpful to use half-halts to balance and soften the horse before applying the aids for the canter strike-off.

I have found that the strike-off is usually a psychological problem for the rider, who is afraid to ride forward into the canter and tries to stop the head coming up by jamming his hands when he goes into the canter.

Problems with the halt usually arise because the rider stops the horse with his hands instead of using his legs and waiting for the halt to come. When too much hand is used the horse invariably fails to halt square, because pulling stiffens the neck, hollows the back and usually stops one hindleg coming up level with the other.

The horse must come into the halt with his hindquarters underneath him. If he is on his forehand, he will lean on the rider's hands, stiffen through the back and resist. The answer is the same as in all other transitions: soften the contact with the hands so that the horse has less to resist against, at the same time help him keep his balance and then use the legs to get the transition to come through from behind.

Another result of too much hand into a halt is for the hindquarters to swing to one side. The horse must be kept straight by keeping an even contact in both hands at the same time that the legs are applied. If he consistently swings to one side, put the leg that side further back as the aids to the halt are applied.

Uneven Contact

Most horses try to take hold of one rein more than the other. Usually they are hard on the left and are said to be 'nice and light on the right'. I find it easier to think of it the other way round; that is, the horse is not taking hold of the right rein. Therefore I encourage him to do so by keeping my right hand still so that he can maintain a light, soft contact and never let it go. At the same time I make it uncomfortable for the horse to catch hold of the left side by moving my left fingers and giving with my left hand, leaving him with nothing to take hold of and fix against on the stiff side. Gradually, over many lessons, the horse will take a more even contact and may even start catching hold of the right and dropping the left as he discovers there is nothing on the left of which to take hold. The approach can then be reversed and reversed again until the horse stays even in both hands.

5

JUMPING

As with dressage, before being able to achieve any level of excellence when jumping, riders must understand the basic principles involved with their equipment, their position and their horse. It is only with this understanding that they can correct and develop their skills in order to achieve a higher standard, which in turn will enable them to compete at a higher level and enjoy their jumping more.

THE SADDLE

The jumping saddle and general purpose saddle are a different shape from the dressage saddle, to help the rider maintain a different balance to do a different job.

Balance

The centre of balance in the forward seat, light seat or jumping seat is a line from the shoulder down through the knee on to the ball of the foot. All the weight should be going down through the knee on to the ball of the foot, stretching the ankle joint and calf muscles as much as possible. It does not matter if you are doing rising trot or canter, if the seat bones are touching the saddle or are out of it, whether you are approaching a fence or jumping it, this weight distribution should not change.

When you are working on the flat, warming up or approaching a fence, if you are to go with the movement of the horse all the time and not fall behind the movement and stop the horse up or jam him up, you

have to be in balance. Therefore you have to conform to the centre of balance for which the saddle was designed, and the shorter you ride the further forward you have to lean with the shoulders in order to maintain the shoulder – knee – ball-of-the-foot centre of balance. To test this, stand on the floor and then lower your elbow to your knee without lifting your heel off the ground. The closer your knee and elbow come together, which equates to the shorter you ride, the further forward you have to lean if you do not want to fall over backwards or if you are riding come behind the movement.

A rider's balance in the light, forward or jumping seat should be second nature to him, just like riding a bicycle, so that he does not have to think about it. Yet many people find it very difficult to find that balance, simply because they have never understood the principle or taken the trouble to develop the base on which they are balanced – the lower leg and the triangle formed by the knee, the ball of the foot and the heel. Instead of stretching the ankle joint so that all the weight is trapped between the heel and the ball of the foot, giving a still and firm base on which to balance, the common fault is to ride on tip-toe, with the heel riding up. It is then very difficult to keep your balance unless you grip with your knees, lower calves and ankles, each of which is wrong.

Developing your lower leg and stretching the ankle joint and calf muscles takes time and concentrated effort; but, like touching your toes, as every day goes past it becomes easier and less painful, and as it gets easier so you develop a stronger leg and become a stronger rider, more secure, better balanced and more able to enjoy your jumping.

I have found it best to concentrate on my lower leg not when I am schooling the horse and thinking of a hundred and one other things at the same time but when I am out on exercise. I often trot along standing up in the stirrups, with my hands off the horse's neck, for five or ten minutes at a time. Often I pull my stirrups a little shorter than normal so that I can feel myself stretching my ankle joint all the time. At every stride in trot or canter I then get the sensation of my heel dropping down and my calf coming up under the barrel of the horse.

Jumping and General Purpose Saddles

Most people handicap themselves before they start by trying to jump in a general purpose saddle. A general purpose saddle is what it says it is: general purpose. In other words, it is a saddle in which you can ride dressage and in which you can jump but which is ideal for neither. Most general purpose saddles are built on the same tree as a dressage saddle, that is, a tree with vertical points. Many saddlers take that same type of tree, put a bigger, more forward-cut flap on it and call it a general purpose saddle, or put an even more forward-cut flap on and call it a jumping saddle.

However, jumping involves an entirely different centre of balance, and therefore we need a different tree, one with forward points. With forward points the stirrup leather hangs vertically when the rider is in the forward or light seat, making it easy for him to keep his balance and develop his lower leg. When the rider is in the same position in a general purpose saddle, the stirrup leather angles backwards, putting more weight on to the knee instead of down through it, encouraging the lower leg to go back and the heel to come up, which in turn makes the rider grip with his knee, lower calf and ankle.

It *is* possible to have a good lower leg position in the forward or light seat in a general purpose saddle – it is just that much more difficult than in the tree and saddle built for the job. I have always found jumping difficult enough as it is without handicapping myself before I start with the equipment on which I am sitting.

THE RIDER'S BALANCE WHEN JUMPING

Riders find that when working on the flat they can get away with their balance not being perfect. They may not always be going with the movement of the horse, as they will inevitably lose their balance from time to time, but the horse will go adequately if not brilliantly. However, as soon as they start jumping they will be in a lot more trouble.

To understand the horse's point of view, I always think of the rider as a monkey sitting in a rucksack on my back. If I come to jump a ditch or a log with my monkey in the rucksack on my back, do I want him to sit still or to be throwing himself forwards, backwards or from side to side? Obviously I am going to be a lot more comfortable and find it a lot easier if he sits still. Now the rider's job is exactly the same as the monkey's. After all, it is the horse, not the rider, who has to jump the fence. All the rider has to do is stay still. If a rider is in balance, with a secure lower leg, the job is easy because there is nothing to do other than absorb the jumping movement through the hips and allow a little more rein over the top of the fence by straightening the arms a little.

Over small fences there is no movement of the head and upper body. It is a popular misconception that the chest has to go down towards the withers. It is in fact the withers that should come up towards the chest. Over a small fence the horse's angle of ascent is quite low and therefore the withers stay a long way from the rider's chest and the rider can give the horse the rein he needs by giving or straightening the arm a little and keeping a straight line between the elbow and the bit. It is only over the bigger show jumps, where the angle of ascent is much steeper, that the withers come right up to the chest and the horse needs so much rein that it becomes necessary to lower the upper body over the top of the fence to give the horse the freedom he needs.

Riding is no different from most other sports in that keeping the head still is of paramount importance. The head is the heaviest part of the body and therefore has a considerable influence on the balance; keeping it still thus makes it easier for the horse to jump the fence. Equally important, while the head is still and up the eyes can be focused all the time on

whatever problem is coming up. The rider is therefore in the 'ballgame' all the time and will have more
time to anticipate and deal with whatever lies ahead.
If his head drops and his eyes go down, not only is he
endangering his balance and taking his eye 'off the
ball', but also sooner or later the unexpected will
happen and he will follow his eyes to the very spot at

The classical American 'crest release' has become
necessary here because of a weak lower leg position
and resultant dip of the upper body over the top of the
fence

which he is looking.

After the take-off, as the horse nears the apex of his jump, the rider's weight should still be on the balls of his feet and he should be bent at the hips and reaching forward with his hands to allow the horse to stretch and use his head and neck. As the horse starts to come down, the rider should begin to sit up, bringing his upper body back, with all the weight still on the balls of the feet to support him on landing. As the horse lands the rider must support him with the reins so that he can regain his balance and move straight away from the fence. The rider must also stay balanced as he lands so that he can stay balanced with the horse as he moves away from the fence.

The most common rider problems are getting left behind over a fence or getting in front of the movement. The usual reasons for the rider getting left behind are that his reins are too long and his weight is too far back on his seat bones. If a rider does find himself left behind, the vital factor is quickly to open the fingers so that the reins can slip through. This will avoid jabbing the horse in the mouth and destroying his confidence.

The most usual problem is getting in front of the movement and therefore out of balance at take-off. If the rider's weight is too far forward, it will make it difficult for the horse to bring his shoulders up, because the rider's weight comes over the shoulders at the second the horse is trying to bring them up off the ground. The inevitable result is a rather flat jump by the horse, who will also probably hit the fence.

Occasionally, getting in front of the movement is caused by the rider throwing himself forward and saying to the horse, 'I'm going to jump the fence', and then hoping the horse comes too. More often though, it is caused by riders being off balance and behind the movement in the approach, with too much weight on the seat bones. If the weight is on the seat bones because the rider cannot accelerate his upper body forward fast enough and at the exact time of lift off, the rider will throw his upper body forward in anticipation of the jump so as not to get left behind; human nature sees to that. The trouble is that as soon as you throw the upper body forward you immediately get in front of the movement, with your weight on the horse's shoulders just as they are leaving the ground.

It is also very important not to get in front of the movement over the top of the fence, because on landing the only ways in which the rider can prevent himself tipping over the horse's front are by putting his hands on the neck for support and by gripping with his calves. The rider will tend to balance himself with his hands on the horse's neck just when the horse needs help to bring his head up. If the calves are used for gripping, the lower legs will swing back and the heels and knees come up as the rider tenses. Then, if anything goes wrong on landing, the lower leg will flip up, and in this position the rider cannot support

the horse as he lands; also, when the lower leg flips back the rider tends to lose his balance and tumble off if the horse slips, pecks, jinks or stumbles on landing, or if he misses the neck with his hands.

Before progressing with training the horse further in his jumping, I have to assume that the rider has taken the time and trouble to develop his lower leg and balance in the forward seat. This fundamental skill is critical to how much progress can be made. If this skill is not established, progress cannot be made from a secure base and the rider will tend to put the horse into trouble as often as, if not more frequently than, he helps him with his education and training over fences.

When jumping a fence there are many things to think about and, as the obstacle looms ever closer, our own balance tends to be fairly low down on the list of priorities in the brain. That is why that balance must become second nature so that the rider can concentrate on the job at hand, which is to make it as easy as possible for the horse to jump the fence.

THE GOLDEN RULES

Going Forward
The first and most vital thing of all to understand is the importance of having the horse going forward. Having the horse in front of the leg or up to the hand are different ways of saying the same thing. Going forward is the desire to go forward, having the horse

going freely from the leg to the hand, the desire to go that little bit faster than is being allowed. I always like to have the feeling that my horses are saying, 'Whoopee, Dad, we're going jumping'.

When that desire to go forward, that desire to get to the fence, is contained by the hand, what you are holding is the power with which you are going to be able to get the horse to the fence and the power which the horse is going to use to jump the fence. I like to think that as long as the desire to go forward is there and I keep it contained, then I am keeping the spring coiled. As soon as I let go, there is nothing to keep the spring coiled and the power is gone. With the young horse, speed is a factor in generating for wardness or power. With the green horse the only

The rider's position over a fence: a good lower leg position and good balance in the jumping seat are crucial in the approach, over the top of the fence and on landing to give the horse the best possible chance to jump the fence

Note the weak lower leg position, necessitating the rider supporting himself on the horse's neck

way to generate that power is to get him going quite fast then, keeping the leg on, slow him down so that you are doing as much as you can to compress the spring. As the horse becomes more trained you can generate the same and more power at a slower speed and with more balance and collection.

Balance

The second point to be continually thinking about is the horse's balance. In dressage we are looking for balance within a frame. In jumping we are simply looking for balance. The hindleg should be coming under the horse as far as possible to take as much weight as possible. The shoulders should be light, coming up off the ground every stride, and the poll and ears should be the highest point of the neck, with the horse's nose out in front of it. I like to think of my horses travelling in an uphill attitude every stride to

make it as easy as possible for them to bring the front end off the ground before they power over the fence.

Following your nose is an old expression and I believe it to be true of horses when jumping. If the horse's nose is up and out, he will be in balance and thinking forward. If his nose is down and in, he will be thinking of leaning and of not going forward.

Leaning is the problem facing most riders. If the horse is allowed to lean on the rider's hand, he stops himself up against the hand, tenses through his back, his hindleg does not come under him and therefore he cannot be going forward. If he is leaning, he cannot be balanced and carrying himself because he is supporting himself on the rider's hand, using it as a fifth leg. Very often riders mistake the weight of contact that comes from leaning for the weight of contact that comes from the desire to go forward. The acid test is to keep freeing the reins. If the horse continues in the same attitude and perhaps just goes a little faster, then he is balanced. If his head goes down when freed, he is not balanced.

A small loss of balance is easily cured by putting

more leg on to bring the hindleg further under and by slightly raising the horse's head. The more habitual leaner needs more drastic action and the rider, still with the leg on, has to bring the horse's head so high that he can no longer lean. Once the horse is carrying himself the rider can drop his hands and put the horse in front of the leg up to the hand again. The process will need repeating until the horse gets into the habit of travelling in a balance most of the time.

As the degree of balance increases, so that balance 'compresses the spring' as the horse takes more and more weight on his hindlegs. Therefore as the training develops and balance improves, so the power that the rider holds in his hands will become softer, and as it becomes softer so that power will become more manageable and the horse more rideable.

Rhythm

Going forward + balance = rhythm, which is like saying 1 + 1 = 2. If the horse is not going forward or is not balanced, then you cannot have rhythm, and without rhythm jumping becomes very difficult. Without rhythm it is difficult to adjust a horse's stride and therefore to influence the point of take-off, and you end up going to the fence on a wing and a prayer with what you have and hoping you will get there or thereabouts.

But if the horse is going forward and is in balance then he will have rhythm, which will enable the rider to keep an even tempo and comfortable length of stride on the approach to the fence. If he is kept in an even rhythm, with an even stride, he should be nicely balanced on his feet and he will find it easy to jump. If the rhythm is lost because either power or balance is lost, then the stride becomes longer and flatter and the horse will either jump low and flat or pop in a little short stride to balance himself before jumping the fence. Similarly, if the rider breaks the rhythm by using too much hand and shortening the strides, the horse can only go straight up and down over the fence or stop.

Waiting for the Stride and the Fence to Come

I believe it is a great mistake for the rider to try to see a stride into the fence. This is because if the rider is thinking about looking for a stride then subconsciously the arms stiffen, the handbrake (the hand) goes on, the accelerator (the leg) comes off, power is lost, the horse stops going forward and the rhythm is lost. When the stride eventually does appear, the rider cannot move the horse to the fence or shorten his stride because there is not enough power or impulsion. For the same reason he cannot shorten the stride without breaking back into trot. What tends to happen is that in the excitement of seeing the stride and the anxiety of getting to the fence, the rider thinks, 'There it is,' sees one-two-three strides to the fence, drops the reins, and loses the balance as well. The horse then either has to make a long, low, flat jump or say, 'No, I cannot jump like that' and put in an extra little short stride to re-balance himself.

Instead, the rider should simply concentrate on keeping the horse going forward, keeping him balanced and maintaining that rhythm all the way to the fence. He should wait for the stride and the fence to come to him and not be anxious to get to the fence. He must think all the time, 'Keep coming, keep coming' rather than 'Where is it? Where is it?' To help me to 'keep coming' all the way to the fence the two things I always have to think about are keeping my leg on and my arm soft and elastic. I keep my leg on to keep the horse going forward, to keep the hindleg coming under and the shoulder up, so that he is balanced. I keep my arm elastic so as not to stop him up or jam him up, thus losing power and impulsion.

Anyone who has ever jumped has a flat spot five, six, seven or eight strides out from a fence. It is the moment when human nature tells you to start looking for a stride. The bigger the fence the greater the pressure and the bigger the temptation to tighten the arm and ease off with the leg. It is the extent to which a rider can control his anxieties in the approach to a fence, and discipline himself to keep the leg on and the arm soft to maintain rhythm whatever the circumstances, that eventually determines how successful a competitor he will be.

WORK ON THE FLAT

Most people love jumping, particularly those who compete, at whatever level, over fences. Very often the whole point of riding is the thrill and excitement of sailing through the air, at one with your horse over an obstacle. That sensation is the good news. The bad news is that unless you are only jumping very small obstacles it is the work on the flat which makes it all possible. This is because the approach to the fence is all-important. If the approach is correct, the size of the obstacle is immaterial, the only limiting factor being the physical ability of the horse you are riding at the time. If the approach is not correct, you need a brave horse or one with a lot of ability to get you over a fence.

The two essentials for the successful negotiation of an obstacle are that the horse is going forward and that he is balanced. Of the two, having the horse going forward is probably the easier to achieve. It is when you try to combine that desire to go forward with balance that life starts to become more complicated.

If you are unable to get the horse going freely away from the leg and up to the hand, there is no point in holding out any great aspirations for your horse as a competition vehicle. If he is not going forward because he is tired, unfit or bored with his place of work, then the remedy is within your grasp. If, however, his temperament and character are so laid-back that he has little ambition to put one foot in front of the other, you may rest assured that his future is neither at the Olympic Games nor even at the local BHS one-day event.

When preparing the horse on the flat for jumping, all the same principles apply as when you are doing dressage – with one notable exception. I have talked at some length in Chapter 2 about the importance of having the horse supple, without lateral stiffness, and of keeping him straight. You cannot get away from those principles, because without them it is impossible to keep the horse going forward and balanced. The exception is that in dressage we need balance within a frame but for jumping all we need is the balance. There are no extra marks for the horse's outline; all that matters is that he should clear the fence.

Therefore in preparation for jumping I concentrate all the time first on keeping the horse going forward and second on keeping the poll and the horse's ears as the highest point of the neck. The horse must not be allowed to lean on my hand but must carry himself all the time. I do not mind how high he carries his head so long as he is taking the contact forward and not down. He must not lean on my inside

leg and fall in around his corners because that, too, is a loss of balance. I am particular about making him step around my inside leg. Similarly, I take a lot of care not to pull the horse around a corner with the inside rein and let the shoulder fall out, because again that results in a loss of balance.

Having got the horse going forward and starting to travel in a balance, not just in straight lines but around the corners as well, I start to get him to lengthen for a few strides, both in trot and in canter, and then come back again, and start to make the turns tighter – all without a loss of balance. The tendency to begin with is for the horse to fall on his head, increasing the weight of contact in the hand when he goes up or comes down a gear. Similarly, the tighter you make the turns, the more likely the shoulder is to fall in or out, with a subsequent loss of balance.

I am meticulous about the horse's balance through all transitions: from walk through trot to canter and back down again, in walk to canter and canter to walk. I try to do a number of exercises, all designed to improve the balance of the horse: shoulder-in at both trot and canter, and canter to halt to rein-back to canter transitions – all aimed at getting as much weight as possible off the forehand and on to the quarters. I try to think of the profile of the horse as being 'uphill', that is, travelling in an attitude in which the quarters are the lowest point, with the outline then going uphill or upwards through the withers to the poll as the highest point.

GRIDWORK

Depending on the amount of building material available, you can build an almost infinite number and variety of grids. Exactly what you build will very much depend on what you are trying to achieve.

Most horses competing in horse trials tend to be free-going and to jump a little flat. Therefore the grids you build would be designed to teach the horse to back himself off an obstacle and to shorten and compress himself between elements, as well as to get him to jump in a rounder outline. On the other hand, the same grid could back off a less enthusiastic jumper so much that it could well stop him.

Before going into more details about what types of grids can be built and what can be done with them, as always I believe it is very important for the rider to have a clear understanding of what he is trying to do.

We spend a lot of time on the flat developing the power and cadence of the working trot. It is that same forward-going powerful trot that is needed when approaching a grid. It is very easy to fall into the trap of thinking that because a distance is short in a line of fences the trot should be slow and under-powered. I believe this to be a fallacy, for if the approach is underpowered the horse will jump long and flat, and find it that much more difficult to jump the fences in a grid where he has really to use himself in order to clear the jumps. If the power is there, he will jump much rounder and find it much easier to handle a short distance.

I use as many trotting poles as are necessary to enable me to come to a grid going forward in a nice regular rhythm. The more onward bound the horse, the more trotting poles are usually required. I like to be able to drop my hands in the trotting poles and leave the rest of the grid to the horse, using just enough leg to keep him going forward and to keep enough power on to enable him to jump the fences easily. The rider then simply has to concentrate on staying balanced himself.

The temptation is to anticipate the jump and get in front of the movement, so unbalancing the horse, or alternatively to have a feel of his back teeth if he is making too much ground between fences. Either way you destroy the whole objective of a grid. The grid is an exercise to make the horse look and think about what he is doing and to use himself over a fence. Sure, the horse may well make a mistake to start with – but it needs to be *his* mistake and he needs to have only himself to blame.

If the rider has been up around his ears or hanging on to his back teeth when he makes a mistake, very often the error will be because the horse has been thinking about what the rider is up to rather than concentrating on the job at hand and the horse will relate the experience more to the rider's over-zealous activity than to his own ineptitude. The rider simply has to keep the horse active and going forward and to sit still so as to let the horse learn from his exercise.

There are so many things to think about when jumping single fences that the rider's position tends to come low down on the list of priorities. Grids are therefore the ideal place to concentrate on your balance and position so that they become second nature to you when jumping out and about.

I very rarely chastise a horse for stopping in a grid. There is the odd occasion when it is merited, for instance if the horse has been down once and then stops because he is thinking about the gate or another horse. But if you start with the premise that you build every grid for the individual horse, if he does stop it is more likely because you have made it too big or too difficult too quickly. The object of a grid is to encourage the horse to jump and use himself, not to frighten him; therefore if he stops, my immediate reaction is to lower the fences and adjust the distances to make it easy again for him to jump, thus restoring his confidence. Similarly, if a young horse tries to run out in a grid, I would take the temptation away by constructing a temporary wing by leaning a pole on top of a stand.

I also try if at all possible never to use heavy poles in a grid. I want the horse to gain confidence, not to hurt himself if things go wrong. In a similar vein, when using parallels in a grid I like to have one end of the back pole resting on the top of the cup so that it falls down very easily. Nothing destroys confidence more quickly than a horse landing on a back bar in a grid.

I nearly always start with one or more trotting poles to a cross-pole. I can then concentrate on the quality of my approach to a very small fence; in addition, the cross-pole helps to keep the horse straight. If the horse is jumping confidently and well, I would then raise it quite quickly. A pole on the ground 9–12ft beyond the cross-pole will help to make the horse lower his head over a fence and jump in a rounder outline. When using a pole on the landing side, never have it closer than 9ft for fear of the horse landing on it and injuring himself.

For the more experienced horse I often progress to the same exercise with a parallel bar. The effect of the parallel bar is to improve the horse's action in front, because he needs to bring his knee higher and his forearm more nearly parallel to the ground in order to clear the back pole. This, combined with the pole on the landing side, really makes a horse drop his head, use his shoulders and round his back over a fence.

Some trainers use a pole on the ground 1ft or 2ft out from under the back pole, again to give the horse something to look at and to encourage him to drop his head. I sometimes try it but I have had limited success with this technique. However, all horses are different and you never know what is going to work for your horse, so it may be worth a try.

When adding additional elements to a grid there are a few very basic rules to follow. Out of trot, the two elements of a bounce should be 9ft apart and out of canter they should be 12ft apart. Out of trot the two elements of a one-stride distance should be 18ft apart and out of canter 21ft.

Hence there are a number of 'classical' grids, the ones most commonly used being those set out below.

I go on increasing the height and spread until the horse is starting to find it difficult. The golden rule is never to reduce the distance between back poles and front poles to less than 18ft.

In a two-stride grid I will often use two placing poles on the ground to start with to stop the horse making too much ground between elements. In fact, whatever grid you are building, the use of placing poles between elements is always a good way of steadying a horse up, of getting him to drop his head and of regulating his stride between fences.

There are a number of other ways in which you can use poles to help your cause. Straightness is always important in a grid, for if a horse is jumping to the left or right, he is evading the question and trying to give himself a bit more room. Guide poles can be used in a number of different ways: on the ground at take-off and/or on landing; one end of a pole resting on top of the fence on the take-off and/or landing side; or simply a diagonal pole from the top of the stand down across the front of the fence.

Extreme care should be taken if you are using poles on the landing side of a fence. Landing on the poles can have serious consequences for both horse and rider. The motto is always to err on the side of caution to begin with and then gradually bring the effect of the pole into play.

Similarly, if you rest a guide pole on top of a pole in a jump, the effect is to jam that top rail of the fence into the cup, creating something near to a 'fixed' obstacle. Again, if anything goes wrong, the consequences can be dire, and so again I often have one end of the top rail resting on the back edge of the cup.

The V is a very useful aid in getting a horse to back off a fence, and this too can be used in a variety of ways: either laid on the ground with the point just on the landing side or with the point resting on top of or just above the top rail. I sometimes use slats or 2in ×

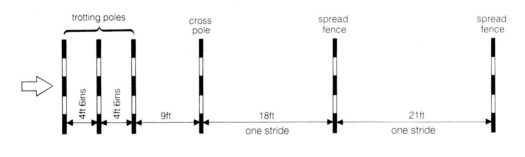

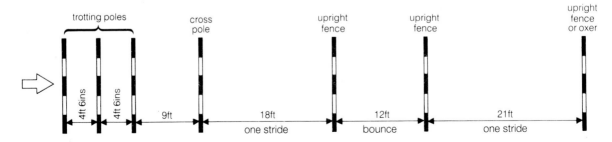

Two examples of classical grids

The whole dressage test should be smooth and flowing. Here King William is looking soft, supple and attentive at Badminton 1991 while Mary Thomson, head held high, glances down to check all is in order

The distance in a bounce into water always rides longer than it walks. It is amazing how quickly horses can stop – often quicker than their riders!

Jacana (Richard Walker) proving that even with a 9ft ditch an open ditch is one of the easiest of all cross-country obstacles to jump: no more than a triple bar without the middle rail

Corners are great time savers. Virginia Leng and Griffin demonstrate how to tackle the problem in perfect balance

Punchestown's famous Irish bank. This rider coming off the bank may be a little bit too much on the defensive, a fault on the right side

The rider, in perfect balance, is already starting to slip the reins in preparation for the big descent

The 'Breitling time piece' set at the top of a hill at Gatcombe

Mark Todd working hard on Welton Greylag to stay with the movement at the same fence

The bigger the jump, the more the rider has to sit up and slip the reins and the further forward the lower leg has to come.
Lucinda Green expecting the worst at Badminton

Steps down and drop fences rarely cause a horse any difficulty. A good lower leg and perfect balance enable Owen Moore to jump right by the white flag with Locomotion Passadena II (William Miflin) in extended trot. Horse and rider in great balance

The pressures of the occasion create a bit too much body movement at the European Championships at Punchestown

Steps up require power and momentum

A pole placed diagonally across the front of the fence prevents the horse, in this case, from drifting to the right. Note that the pole is in a cup and not wedged behind the upright. With a groundline this also works well. It is slightly safer if the diagonal pole goes from the cup down between the two parallel rails

A pole resting diagonally across the top of a wide parallel will improve the action of the horse's front legs and stop him touching down in the middle. Note the back pole resting on the edge of the cup for safety because of the extra weight on the poles in the cups caused by the diagonal rail

2in or 2in × 4in rails as well. The advantage of the slats is that they can be used in an X or a V in the horizontal as well as the vertical plane. Also, because they are very light they do the job with much less risk of hurting the horse.

Whatever grid you are building and however many poles you are using in whatever position, the most important rule about working in grids is to quit while you are ahead. By this I mean stop before the horse gets tired, before the fence becomes too big or a distance too short. As a trainer you can see and as a rider you can feel when a horse is starting to have to make a real effort; that is the moment to stop or even lower the fence. To come one more time or to go up one more hole is always fatal.

Remember also that as the fences become higher the distance between them effectively becomes shorter. Therefore if you want to make the horse use himself more, you always have two options open to you: one is to raise the pole, the other to shorten the distance. When shortening the distance I do not like going more than 6in at a time, so that the horse learns

little by little. If you shorten a distance too far or too quickly, you will end up jamming the horse up so that he cannot use himself. Obviously you should stop before getting to that point.

QUALITY OF JUMP

The irritating thing about jumping is that if you do the simple things correctly it is really very easy. How difficult it is, though, sometimes just to do those simple things, particularly if you are inhibited by the fence or if the pressure is on! However, the answer is always in the Three Golden Rules. After every fence ask yourself: Was the horse going forward, was the horse balanced? If the answer to both is 'Yes,' then you had rhythm; if the answer is 'Could have been better,' then so could your rhythm. That only leaves you to ask yourself whether you maintained your rhythm to the fence or whether you were 'picking' at the horse while looking for a stride. If you maintained your rhythm, for certain you had a good jump; if you did not, you may or may not have been

Poles placed in a V shape help to get a horse to back off a fence, causing this horse to go very high in the air and the author to release too much rein

lucky and left the fence up.

I find when teaching that very often the answer I get to one or all three questions is, 'Well, it was okay,' or 'It was all right.' The answer to that is always, 'And you had an okay or all-right sort of a jump.' This is always the critical point: just how hungry are you to get better? If 'all right' is good enough, you will only ever be an all-right sort of rider. If you get mad at yourself because it could and should have been better, you are on the road to success.

Because in horse trials we never jump more than 3ft 11in, the great temptation is to come under-powered or not going forward enough to the fences. In other words, because the fences are relatively small you can often 'get away' with using too much hand and not enough leg. The trouble is that you can only get away with things for so long, and you tend to get caught out at the very highest level of the sport and when the pressure is on, no matter what the level.

If you were coming down to a 5ft fence you would definitely feel the urge to have full power on. Logically, if you have enough power to jump 5ft, think how easy it is going to be to jump 4ft. It was not until I spent some time show jumping internationally that I really started to comprehend this and to understand what I had been getting away with. I would recommend anyone in horse trials to take every opportunity they can to jump bigger fences. It is the acid test of just how good your technique is or whether you are kidding yourself into believing that you are better than you really are.

RELATED DISTANCES

I enjoy related distances as they are always a test of whether or not you are really on the boil. Strictly speaking, anything over 12yds (two strides) and under 30yds is a related distance, though I believe that once fences are more than 20yds apart their relativity becomes less and less because you have so much time to adjust and start again.

When training at home I normally use a distance

Slats used in an X in the horizontal. Being light, they are unlikely to hurt a horse if he makes a mistake. They are another way to help keep a horse straight and to improve the action of the legs and the shape of the horse in the air

of 19yds, which I find is a nice comfortable four strides. I often find that to come down in a good, regular, even four strides, when I have to do nothing, is the most difficult thing to achieve. I feel much happier if I am doing something.

Having gone down in four strides I then practise going down the same distance in five and six strides and on some horses perhaps even seven. After that I have to cheat and put a bend in the line. If taking a whole stride out is too much for a horse at the beginning, just keep reducing the distance by a foot at a time but still keep putting in the same number of strides. That way you can get to the maximum the horse can achieve for his present state of training in the easiest and kindest possible way.

To add the extra strides it is necessary to sit up much more quickly than normal after the first fence so that you can lose the distance in the first stride after you land. It is always this first stride that is the important one, whether you are trying to gain or lose distance. If you can lose the distance at the beginning, then you can have the maximum number of regular strides before the next jump and therefore have the best chance of jumping it. The worst thing that can happen is still to be trying to lose distance when you reach the second fence, because then more often than not you will finish by stopping the horse at the fence or your efforts to lose ground will result for certain in the horse losing power instead of increasing it in the last stride.

The great temptation when trying to shorten a stride to lose distance is to use only the hand. The truest thing that was ever said to me about jumping was when I was told in the Pony Club, 'Remember, boy, for every one in the kisser, the horse needs two in the guts.' In other words, whatever you do with your hand, you need twice as much leg. This is particularly true when trying to shorten the stride, because if you only use hand, you stop the horse up and jam him up in his back instead of bringing the hindleg under and increasing the balance and power by keeping the leg on.

The business of adding strides sounds very simple; it is, but the trouble is that there are a couple of prerequisites. First, you must have rhythm coming to the first fence, otherwise you are more in the business of adjusting to the mess you made of the first fence than anything else; second, you must be able to stay in balance with your horse over the fence. If you are not in balance over the first fence, you cannot possibly get your weight into position quickly enough to have any real influence on the all-important first stride after landing.

If you land supporting yourself with your hands on the horse's neck, it will be at best the second stride after landing before you have any positive influence on proceedings, and if you fall forward after landing, it could well be the third or sixth stride before you are back in the 'ballgame'.

Another common fault is to sit up and hold in the first stride only to fall or be pulled forward in the second stride after landing. Obviously this too defeats the object of the operation. The art is to sit up on the descent over the first fence so that as the horse lands you are already in a position to say 'wooah' or 'steady' to the horse. Then in the first and subsequent strides you can say 'steady' again and soften until you have the lost the distance required.

The 'softening', keeping the elbow elastic, is as important as the 'steadying'. If you just hold you jar the horse and lose power; if you stay soft it enables the horse to keep working behind, going forward and maintaining power while you are losing ground. The great riders of the world are great for many reasons but none more pertinent than that they always keep their horses going forward and never jar them up, so their horses always retain their power and are always able to use their ability. You will always see a horse jumping well under a rider whose elbow is constantly flexing.

The other option in a related distance is to take a stride out and lengthen between elements. This is always more difficult as the danger is always that you lose balance. The technique is to kick as though you are kicking the horse as he lands and again in the first stride so that you move away from the first fence with a longer than normal stride. You then keep going until sufficient ground has been gained so that you can sit up and restore the balance in the last strides before jumping the second fence.

The common fault is to try to make the ground with the shoulders and get in front of the movement. That way you not only lose the balance but the power also and it is then very difficult to get both back before jumping again. The leg is the accelerator and the secret of lengthening the stride is for the rider to stay in balance and sink the heel to get maximum power from the legs. Again this is very difficult if a rider has not taken the trouble to 'develop' his lower leg.

Once the art of gaining or losing ground has been mastered, though, solving any distance problems set by modern-day course designers is a simple matter.

DOUBLES/COMBINATIONS

Just as rhythm is critical when jumping a single fence and crucial when negotiating fences on a related distance, so it becomes vital when jumping doubles or combinations, particularly when you only have a one-stride distance. With only one stride between fences everything happens very quickly and there is very little time to adjust between elements if things have gone awry at the first part. Therefore a good jump in is always essential.

Assume though, for a moment, that things have gone wrong and you have jumped in too far, too fast or flat. You can help to save the situation by starting to sit up while you are still in mid-air so that you can help the horse to steady and balance himself between elements and thereby help him to take a shorter stride. This is exactly the same technique as that used when looking to lose ground in a related-distance situation.

Similarly, if you drop in over the first element too slowly, too steeply or with not enough power, you should kick the horse as he is landing and again in his first stride in order to make up as much ground as possible to the second element. Again this is the same technique as that used when trying to gain ground or take a stride out in a related distance.

In both cases, though, the rider's balance is again critical. The rider must stay in balance and not bump down on to the saddle between fences. The weight coming back in this way will tend to make the horse hollow, and even if he clears the next fence with his front legs the chances are that he will have it behind.

RIDING A LINE

Being able to ride on a line is an essential skill for the modern competitor to master. It means that you can jump fences on angles and jump to one side or the other of a fence to save time or to give you a better line or better ground to jump on. Across country its implications are even greater but here we will just confine ourselves to the show jumping.

Again, the essential is rhythm. To jump a fence successfully on an angle or to jump a fence right next door to the wing, you have to think about coming on a holding stride so that you can hold the horse to the exact point at which you want to jump the fence. In short, the long stride is not an option. If you give too much with the reins, you allow the horse the opportunity to run down or run out at the fence. If you maintain your rhythm and hold the horse to the point at which you are hoping to jump, it becomes a simple matter. If you start pushing and shoving the horse to the fence, if you are anxious to get there or leave the horse off the fence, he has the opportunity to duck the issue. Some of our more honest friends may jump the fence anyway, no matter what you do; unfortunately, though, it is always on the big day that you get let down.

When training a horse to jump at angles I often use a figure of eight; I start by jumping just off the straight line and then increase the angle little by little. The secret though is to have the horse fully 'in front of the leg' 'up to the hand' all the time.

TURNING IN THE AIR

It is amazing how much time you can save if a horse turns well in the air, for you can land facing the direction you want to go rather than taking two or three strides to turn after a fence. I've never enjoyed giving the opposition that much of an advantage! Ask for just a little at a time, but be increasingly positive. When in the air, put your weight on the foot on the side of the direction you want to go and at the same time open your hand out away from the withers on the same side. The hand will help turn the horse's head and 'show' which way you are intending to go, and the horse will go that way also to compensate for the shift in weight to that side.

It often takes some time to teach a horse to turn well in the air. To train a horse I will jump a fence several times, always asking him to jump and turn the same way. This would be a bad thing to do with a young horse because it might become a habit, but when practising eventually the horse will start to anticipate what is going to happen and start turning

Teaching the horse to turn in the air. The rider puts weight on the foot on the side of the direction he wants to go, at the same time opening the hand out away from the withers

before he lands, thereby turning in the air.

I believe this is an essential skill and something that a competition rider should teach every horse sooner or later. Even if you have no great ambitions in competition, it is amazing how much easier it is to jump into a lane out hunting if the horse will turn in the air.

TURNING UP TO A FENCE

In all turns the most important aid you have is your eyes. Making a turn on a horse is just like driving a corner in a motor-car, where you are always looking ahead, first for the apex of the corner and second for the exit. Wherever your eyes go the horse will follow; how easily he follows your eyes will depend on how

well trained he is.

Again, just as with a motor-car, you must accelerate through your turns so that you always come out of a corner both balanced and above all going forward. To do this effectively the rider must first understand the principle of driving round a corner in a car (see diagram).

In a car you brake coming into a corner, set the car, make the turn and accelerate through the corner and away. On a horse you slow down to the speed at which you can make the turn, keeping the leg on to keep the horse balanced, make the turn, keeping both outside hand and leg on, and then come out of the corner going forward into your next fence.

In a car if you do it wrong and turn too early, you hit the apex too soon and finish up running out of road. On a horse if you cut in too soon, you finish up

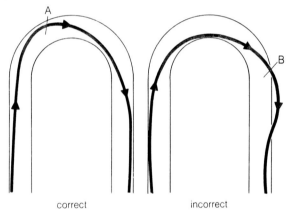

correct   incorrect

Making a turn, whether in a racing car or on a horse, is identical

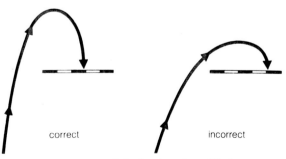

correct   incorrect

Making the turn when applied to jumping a fence. Whether you are in a car or on a horse you can accelerate from point A, either out of the turn, or into the fence. In both cases, at point B the brake is on because you are running out of road in the one instance and about to miss the fence in the other still trying to make the turn (run out of road) when you get to the fence. When this happens you inevitably finish up with too much hand (brake) and not enough leg (accelerator).

One of the reasons why your eyes are so important as an aid is that they enable you to make the turn smoothly, and avoiding running out of road. But, assuming that you are looking ahead and have plotted a smooth curve, you must then concentrate on keeping the leg on throughout the turn. This is very important so that you do not lose any power in the turn but come out of the corner with enough power and going forward sufficiently to jump whatever fence is coming up.

The next thing to think about is the balance. It is essential that you do not pull the horse round the corner with the inside rein. This always brings the head round, causing the shoulder to fall out and balance and power to be lost. The key is always to keep the leg on and to keep hold of the outside rein so that the outside rein brings the horse round the corner. I always think of making the turn in a series of straight strides so that I do not get too much bend and lose everything out through the shoulder. Nearly as important is not to let the shoulder fall in, because again if the horse falls in around the corner, with his head to the outside, then of course the balance is lost. As with working on the flat, this tendency must be counteracted by more bend and more inside leg.

The key to successful jumping lies in the approach. The quality of the jump you get is directly proportional to the quality of the approach. If the approach has power and rhythm, then the horse will jump to the best of his ability. If that power and rhythm are lost in the turn before the fence, normally the fence comes up too quickly for you to get things back on plan in time and you are in trouble. That is why it is so important to understand the mechanism of the turn and to train and train at improving the quality of the turns so that you come out of *every* corner ready to jump whatever is in front of you. It doesn't happen automatically because a horse finds it very easy to fall out of balance and lose power in a turn. Horses need to be trained to turn well in front of a fence and it is something that needs to be worked on regularly, for the better the horse gets at it, the shorter you can turn up to your fences and the more time you are going to save.

PROBLEMS

Jumping Crooked

If the horse jumps to one side, rest one end of a pole on top of the wing and the other on the ground. Alternatively you can rest one end on top of the fence and the other on the ground on the side to which he tends to jump. In both cases ride close to the pole. Alternatively, the jump can be raised on the side to which the horse is veering.

Jumping Flat

Jumping flat is a common problem with the onward-bound event horse, and much of my gridwork is designed to train the horse to take shorter strides so that he learns to back off and round himself over a fence. It is easier to teach the horse to compress himself through the use of poles, and the gradual shortening of distances between them, than for the rider to push with his legs and contain with his hands, which starts the pushing/pulling syndrome.

A useful grid for the horse who jumps flat consists of trotting poles to the first fence, followed by a pole on the ground before the next and after this second fence another pole on the ground, so that the horse has to keep looking at the ground. When looking at the pole he has to drop his head, bring his shoulders up and round himself in the air.

This pole on the ground must be halfway between two fences separated by one non-jumping stride. It must not be placed where the horse could land on it. If you are in any doubt, start with it 12ft from the first fence and, when you have found out where the horse lands and are confident that he is not going to land on it, gradually bring it back to a minimum of 9ft from the fence.

The parallel is another good aid to making a horse use himself. Start with a low, small one and gradually make it wider. As long as it is approached slowly and the horse is made to take off close to it, he will have to use himself to make the spread. A parallel can be incorporated into a grid and be gradually increased in width. A grid of three parallels with at least 18ft between any two is an effective means of getting a horse to use himself, but it is best to build up to this gradually with very low fences and trot into them at first.

Another useful trick is to put a pole diagonally across the top of a parallel. This has the effect of making the horse drop his head to look at it. Again, to do this he has to round himself.

A series of bounces is also useful. Four, five or even six fences of gradually increasing height can be set with the bounce distance of 9ft between each of them.

All these devices will help a horse to use himself over the fence, but before he can do this he must learn to approach at an even pace, without rushing. A bad technique is difficult to correct if the approach is unbalanced and fast because the horse will be on his forehand and approaching the fence with long flat strides, from which he can only make a long flat jump. The rounder, more forward and fuller the canter, the better the balance and the more chance the horse has to throw an athletic jump and to use himself.

Rushing

A horse often starts to rush into his fences because he has not been going forward enough. As he approaches he panics because he does not feel he has enough impulsion to get over the obstacle. Many horses stop rushing if they are ridden more forward into the fences, for then they find there is no need to rush. The cause of the worry has been removed and they start to acquire the confidence to wait for the fence to come to them.

If rushing has become a habit, the best way to get the horse to relax and jump more calmly is to use trotting poles and gridwork. One of the most useful grids for this purpose is trotting poles followed by a cross-bar, with a bounce stride to the next fence, one stride to the next and a bounce stride to the next, the thought being that the bounces will keep backing a horse off and stop him from getting quicker and quicker.

Poles placed in a V shape on the fences also help.

An exercise to encourage accurate riding and to train the horse to jump where he is pointed. Three bins side by side are quite easy, so much so that the author has got a little in front of the movement . . .

. . . two are more difficult

In the above grid, start by putting them on the fence going into the last bounce (the second fence), then put another V at the fence before the penultimate bounce. Poles placed in this upside down V shape help whenever a horse tends to run into the bottom of a fence. They help him to back off because he is reluctant to run himself up under the point of the V.

Before jumping single fences, keep circling until the horse relaxes. Put up a large number of small fences in a field, keep jumping them, but circle or go back to the walk whenever he starts to rush. I have spent many hours with many horses circling in front of fences and then coming to a fence off a short approach to try to keep the horse relaxed and convince him in his own mind that there is nothing to worry about and that it is in fact easier to jump off a controlled and relaxed stride. Make sure that in his flat work he is not running through his bridle. Until he can be ridden forward with the leg rather than being restrained by the hand it is best to stop jump-

ing and concentrate on the work on the flat.

Running Out

If the horse runs out to the right, do not pull the left rein as this will only result in the shoulder falling further out to the right. Instead keep the horse straight, which means keeping hold of the right rein as well as the left.

This is very difficult for the rider to understand, because every instinct tells one to pull on the left rein. But the rider must keep the horse straight with the right hand and leg before using the left hand. It is vital to keep the legs on and to hold the horse to the fence without pulling the horse's head round to the left.

Keep checking on the golden rules: that is, that the horse is going forward with balance and the rider is waiting for the fence to come to him. If the horse is going forward with the rider keeping hold of the reins, then he cannot run out. His only evasion will

V rails help the horse to jump a single bin and improve his action

It is surprising how quickly the horse becomes good at it

be to refuse. If the horse stops with his nose on the fence, that is a different problem. But if he runs by a fence, you have no chance of jumping it. I always used to feel that I had been half asleep and not concentrating if ever I allowed a horse to run by a fence.

Refusing

The first thing is to ask why the horse stopped: whether he was being stubborn, was frightened or confused, or did not have a good approach.

If the approach was wrong, then it is up to the rider to ask himself if he kept to the golden rules, and not to get cross with the horse – in fact quite the opposite if the rider did not give the horse a fair chance to jump the fence. If the horse was being stubborn, the remedy will depend on his character. If he was not cooperating or was pulling your leg, he deserves to be chastised. If a smack makes him worse, then he is unlikely to be a successful competition horse as he will be the type to let you down whenever you have to ask a qustion with any force.

To successfully punish a horse who stops, you must hit him the instant he refuses. It is too late after he has turned away. He must still be facing the fence, otherwise he will not associate the stop with the punishment.

When approaching a fence after a stop, give the horse a couple of slaps down the shoulder to provide extra encouragement. It is no use hitting him behind the saddle within five strides of a fence, because he will go away from the whip and usually run out. There are very few riders in the world good enough and quick enough to hit a horse behind the saddle in the last five strides before a fence. The rider can slap the horse down the shoulder going into a fence whenever he feels impulsion is dying and the horse might stop. The voice can also be used to give extra encouragement.

If the horse is stopping because he is frightened, return to jumping smaller fences and then gradually increase the height as his confidence is restored. Again if the horse is genuinely scared there is no point in getting cross with him.

In nine out of ten cases the refusal is due to the rider. Either the horse was not expecting to jump, was not going forward or was not kept in balance, or the rider did not wait for the fence to come to him. Any one of these reasons can lead to the horse losing confidence and starting to stop.

Backing off the Fence Excessively

When a horse backs off a fence it is important to keep the contact and to keep the leg on as strongly as you can. The problem is normally due to a crisis in confidence, so return to jumping smaller fences, or with a young horse get a lead from a more reliable jumper. Hunting, or jumping in company over small fences, is another good solution.

The rider must be 100 per cent committed to jumping the fence. If the rider is not sure, his lack of confidence will soon be conveyed to the horse. This makes the horse lose confidence and back off.

Always try to avoid situations where a horse could lose his confidence. As soon as he has to make an excessive effort over the fences, lower them and finish the jumping session over some smaller obstacles.

When a horse starts to back off a fence the instinctive reaction of most riders is immediately to start kicking or shoving with the hands. For certain to keep the leg on is correct but to let go of his head is a cardinal sin because suddenly you are releasing any power you had left and letting the balance go. The inevitable result will be a stop. When a horse backs off a fence the rider becomes committed to having an extra stride if power and balance are to be maintained, so the secret is to keep hold with the hands and stay soft in the arm, have the extra stride and pop over the fence.

EQUIPMENT TO HELP SOLVE PROBLEMS

Draw-reins

Used in the correct way, draw-reins can be a great help; used in the wrong way, they may have disastrous results. I think of them as being like the curb rein on a double bridle. The important point is not to use them for more than a few days in succession and not to pull back on the draw-reins but to use the legs to ride forward into a contact that is always soft and giving.

Draw-reins are useful when a horse is consistently going above the bit in the strike-off. They can help to solve the problem but, I repeat, should only be used for a few days, certainly not more than a week, otherwise they become like a crutch and you have an instant reversion as soon as they are taken off.

They can also be used for some jumping problems, but only when they are attached as in the photograph – that is, from the bottom of the girth, not the sides – and only over low fences. They are difficult to use when jumping because with double the length of rein the rider has to give much more rein over the fence. That is why it is only safe to jump very small fences in draw-reins. Over a bigger fence, when the rider has to give a lot of rein, it is very difficult to give enough with the draw-rein. Their most valuable use is on a horse who puts his head in the air and rushes at his fences. Draw-reins can help the horse to realize that he can stay in the same frame and still jump the fence.

Market Harborough

I seldom use the Market Harborough. Sometimes though it can be a useful progression from draw-reins. Because the action is not so severe you can jump a bigger fence with the Market Harborough on and it can be a useful transition between draw-reins and a running martingale.

Chambon

Attached so that it runs from the girth, between the horse's legs, up to the bit and over the poll, the chambon is of value on the lunge to encourage the horse to drop his head and stretch it down and away both in trot and canter. Very occasionally I ride a difficult horse with the chambon on to warm him up, loosen him up and encourage him to stretch long and low. I have also sometimes used it over very small fences with a horse who is fighting me all the time and rushing his fences. With the chambon he is fighting himself when he puts his head up and rushes. Very often this fact, combined with the pressure on the poll, will get him to relax and start to drop his head in front of a fence.

The chambon. I have always had the most success using the chambon from the girth through the bit to the poll. Some people, though, use it from the girth, through the rings on the poll and back down to the bit. It is an excellent aid on the lunge to encourage a horse down and away. I have also used it when riding to very small fences to assist in maintaining a rhythm and stopping a horse throwing his head in the air and rushing at fences. Extreme caution is needed if you are riding with a chambon. Always start with it too loose rather than on the tight side

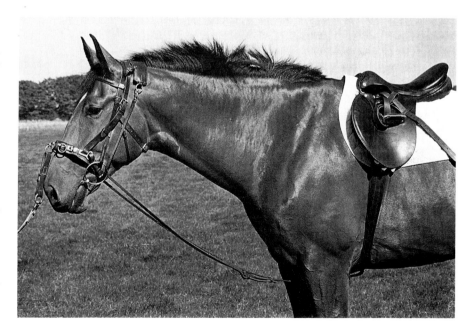

6

CROSS-COUNTRY

The successful cross-country rider must have a good sense of balance, co-ordination and feel, together with some courage and determination. He must want to get to the other side of a fence at all costs, yet at the same time have the self-discipline to work on technique. It helps to start the sport when you are young, because then the learning comes naturally. Starting later in life means that you always tend to do things by numbers in a somewhat pedestrian manner instead of anticipating and reacting instinctively.

The cross-country has always been my favourite part of horse trials. It evokes the greatest extremes of feelings in terms of fear and exhilaration and yet it need not be dangerous. There are obviously risks involved if you travel at 25mph on half a ton of horse over 4ft of fixed timber, but those risks can be minimized if you have a thorough understanding of what you are trying to do. All that cross-country riding is, is show jumping – but 5, 10 or 15mph faster than in the show ring. The principles of jumping the fences are exactly the same

That is a profound statement, and I deliberately used the words show jumping because the whole emphasis of cross-country riding must be on the jumping of the fences. We have to make a few minor adjustments to cater for the extra speed, but we must do everything we can to avoid hitting the fences. Too many people think that cross-country riding is about galloping at fences and big stand-offs, but nothing could be further from the truth. Like dressage and show jumping, riding across country is both an art

and a science.

As always, I believe in starting with the rider, his position and resultant balance. The balance in the forward seat is just as important across country as it is in the show jumping – some would say more so because that balance is now directly linked to the safety with which you are going to jump the cross-country fences. Therefore, to start with the rider must understand the mechanics of the forward seat.

RIDING SHORT ENOUGH

I discussed in Chapter 5 how in show jumping we must ride at the length at which we find it easiest to maintain our own balance, while at the same time keeping the horse going forward and balanced. Across country it is different. Now we must ride as short as we dare. Why? The experts at galloping are the jockeys. Why do the flat-race boys ride with their elbows and knees together? Because that is the position in which they have the greatest strength, and the stronger they are the better able they are to keep the horse balanced, and the more balanced the horse the faster it will run and the more likely it will be to win the race. National Hunt jockeys ride a little longer because they have fences to negotiate, but they ride as short as they dare for the same reason. In horse trials we ride a little longer again, because of the drops, water, coffins and more technical fences, but we, too, must ride as short as we dare to give us the control we need when galloping at speed.

Remember that in the forward seat the knee acts as the pivot. The greater the distance between the knee and the elbow the easier it is for the horse to pull the rider about, making the rider less effective. The shorter that distance, in other words the shorter you ride, the stronger and more effective you become. Think of it like a spanner, with the jaws of the spanner being at your knee and the handle at your elbow. The longer the handle the more the leverage, so the further the elbow is from the knee the more leverage the horse has got to pull you out of position. With flat-race jockeys, who ride with the knee and elbow together, the horse has no leverage and that is why even at very light weights jockeys are able to control and keep balanced large Thoroughbred horses at extreme speeds.

The majority of people riding across country ride too long, either because they have never been told about or do not understand the mechanics of the forward seat, or because they misguidedly believe that it is unsafe to shorten their stirrups. As a rough guide, I like to see the knee just coming out of the front of the saddle when a rider is walking around at the start. Then, as soon as the starter says 'Go', the rider stands up and the knee comes back in behind the knee roll and that is where it stays until the finish. Obviously this can vary a little, according to the length of the rider's thigh and the cut of the saddle, but as a rule of thumb it is pretty accurate.

FINDING YOUR BALANCE

Your balance in the forward seat must be like riding a bicycle: you should not have to think about it. Having got yourself riding at the correct length, the next thing to do is to stand up at the halt, with your knee firmly wedged in behind the knee-roll and your

The author in the forward seat going uphill at canter: what surprises a lot of people is how far forward your weight has to be before you are correctly in balance. When going uphill the head and shoulders have to be even closer to the horse's ears in order for the rider to maintain his balance relative to gravity and level ground

hands off the horse's neck. Move about in this position so that you feel totally comfortable and relaxed, then go off in walk and then trot, all the time standing up, all the time keeping your hands away from the horse's neck. This is an exercise you can easily do while out hacking. Ride out at your cross-country length and trot for twenty minutes, standing up in the stirrups and with your hands off the horse's neck. And you thought you were fit and had a good forward seat! When you can go for twenty minutes without your legs and back begging for mercy and without losing your balance, then I will give it to you.

Having mastered the balance in trot, go through the same exercise in canter. Be sure that you can keep your balance at canter without supporting yourself with your hands on the horse's neck and without supporting yourself on the horse's mouth – in other words on a loose rein. If you can feel your backside touching the saddle every stride, you are not in a true balance. Your bottom should be still and the knees acting as the shock absorbers. Watch the jockeys next time there is racing on television.

What surprises a lot of people is how far forward your weight has to be before you are correctly in balance. To prove it to yourself stand on the ground and, keeping your heels on the floor, lower your elbow to your knee without losing balance.

I would recommend any aspiring horse trials rider to go and ride 'work' in a racing yard. Where better to perfect your forward seat than with the professionals? If you are having difficulty finding your balance, try riding very short like the flat-race jockeys. You think it will be more difficult, but actually it is easier because the shorter you ride the lower your centre of gravity and the easier it is to find your balance.

Remember, too, that the horse will be very grateful if you take the time and trouble to develop a good forward seat. How pleased he will be on the four and a half miles of cross-country at a three-day event if his load is still and not bumping up and down on his back, and how much faster he will be able to go if all his energies can be directed into galloping and jumping, rather than having to make continual allowances for the bumpety-bump on his back.

Also, the stiller the rider, the easier it becomes to keep the horse balanced and galloping faster. The shorter the stirrups the stronger the rider, and therefore the more control the rider has, which in turn means shorter braking distances and less time spent balancing the horse in front of the fences; and of course this means faster times for less wear and tear on the horse.

Apart from the length we ride, the only other difference across country is our balance when we land over a fence. This is one of the very few times when we want to be behind the movement of the horse. As the horse reaches the top of the jump, the rider must start to sit up and push the lower leg forward so that when the horse makes impact with the ground, the lower leg is there to support the upper body. If the rider's position is secure he can in turn give support to the horse as he lands at speed over a fence or down a drop. Then in the first stride after landing the rider can collapse the hips to get the weight forward again and up over the knees, while at the same time picking the horse up and moving him away from the fence.

Again, this skill is not a nicety, it is an essential part of being able to cross the country with safety, but it does have the prerequisite of being able to sit still over a fence. If you cannot stay in balance in the approach, over the top of the fence and on landing, in the show jumping, you cannot get the weight back far enough and quickly enough to come behind the movement on landing when going across country. So many riders get in front of the movement on take-off and land supporting themselves on their hands or the horse's neck. When the horse slips or jinks or the hands miss the neck there can be only one result.

Eighty per cent of all falls across country are a case of unseated rider rather than of the horse falling, and the majority of those are because riders have landed in front of the movement instead of behind it. Nowadays people laugh at the old-fashioned hunting seat and in many cases in those days people did come behind the movement in the extreme. But as with so many things with horses we have much to learn from our predecessors. They had the right idea; today we have merely refined the art.

CROSS-COUNTRY TRAINING

I have never been a great believer in doing a lot of cross-country schooling. Having said that, you do need to familiarize the horse with ditches, water and banks before he goes to his first one-day event.

I have always believed that the most important thing is to have the horse jumping really well over show jumps before asking him to go across country. There are many people who are quite happy to go and jump cross-country fences at 3ft 6in when they are still struggling to clear show jumps at 3ft 3in. I do not belong to that school. I am only happy to gallop at 3ft 6in of fixed timber if my horse is jumping confidently over a 4ft fence that will knock down. I have always found that if I have had a horse that is competing regularly and successfully in Foxhunters, then a BHS Novice horse trials holds few fears.

Remember that when we are jumping the cross-country fences we are trying to do all the same things we were doing in the show ring, going through the same routines, only just going a little bit faster. The shape (or rather profile) of most of the cross-country fences is identical to the corresponding show jumps, with uprights, parallels, triple bars and so on. A pheasant feeder is equivalent to a hog's back, a run-stable rail or a Tidworth to a Swedish oxer, an open ditch to a Liverpool – and so it goes on. I simply make sure that my horses have no inhibitions about water, deep ditches, banks and drops and then I am ready to go.

HUNTING

I find hunting particularly useful for the horse who is indifferent about his cross-country fences. The enthusiast does not need hunting but it definitely helps to fire up the appetite of the more lethargic individual and helps teach horses to look after themselves and handle the unexpected. Few horses who have been well hunted need special schooling over cross-country fences. The hunting field is the ideal place to teach the young horse to be well mannered, to handle himself over all types of terrain and to take on a great variety of little fences, including ditches, drops and water.

In the hunting field the horse can learn to gallop, jump and cope with the unexpected in an environment which he enjoys. If he can be settled when doing this, and learn not to pull all day, then he is unlikely to have any difficulties at horse trials.

Where the young horse is concerned I always treat hunting as part of his educational process, rather than trying to be at the front of the field having a great time. I try to keep him away from the crowds and avoid the hurly burly, especially at gateways. I do not let him gallop flat out across fields but canter him well within himself and try to keep him out of trouble by picking the best places to jump and the best going.

The young horse should have only short days. It is better to have a larger number of short days than one or two long ones because it is when a horse is tired that the risk of injury is greatest. If possible my young horses hunt once a week, progressing to three times a fortnight as they get older. This is the best possible preparation a horse can have for cross-country at horse trials.

ALTERNATIVES TO HUNTING

There are a few horses whose temperaments are unsuitable for hunting in that they get 'drunk' on the galloping, jumping and company, never settle and become more and more unrideable. Hunting would not help their education. They are normally the high-couraged horses, who find the dressage in horse trials far more of a problem than the cross-country fences. There is no point in taking these individuals hunting but they still need experience of travelling and going to different environments: take them instead to hunter trials, or just cross-country schooling. This will give them some experience of being with other horses and give the rider the chance to try to settle them at an early stage in their careers. In areas where there are no opportunities to go hunting then there is no choice but to take young horses to hunter trials, team chases and similar competitions.

Those horses who are not very forward going and lack confidence in their jumping, and the more laid-back characters, can derive great benefit from novice team chases and pairs hunter trials, where they can be given a lead by a more experienced horse.

If hunter trials are part of your horse's introduction to horse trials, be sure to go round keeping your horse working well within himself. Try to ensure that he enjoys his first outing and find a more experienced horse to give him a lead. The most important factor is to keep the young horse on the bridle wanting to go. If he gets tired and wants to slow

down, do not be too proud to pull up. You just have to get him fitter before the next outing.

CROSS-COUNTRY FENCES

With young horses who are bold and have been hunted there is little need for any special work over cross-country fences before a hunter trial or horse trial. But with any that have not been hunting and are rather cautious it pays to practise over some schooling obstacles.

Some horses might take an aversion to water, ditches, steps or drops and will then have to be jumped over as many small versions of the problem fence as possible. However, riders who have not been able to hunt or go to team chases or hunter trials can construct most of the fences easily enough at home using poles and stands. It is surprising, too, how many fences can be found in local fields and woods and even on the side of the road.

The distance in each part of this double bounce is 15ft, a comfortable forward-going distance across country. Double bounces are always deceptive though. Because the horse loses power in the first part he needs to jump the first element a bit quicker and more powerfully than the rider would normally require in order to have enough energy to jump the third element. Here the rider was a little tight to the first element, requiring the horse to stretch a little over the second and third part

The secret of cross-country training is to build up the horse's enthusiasm and confidence, so start over small fences and only jump bigger ones once the horse is jumping the little ones for fun. If you are in doubt about a schooling fence, do not jump it. Schooling half-heartedly over cross-country fences always ends in tears.

Water

Jumping into water is not natural for a horse, therefore the first thing a rider must do is to get rid of the horse's natural inhibitions about walking into water where the bottom cannot be seen and could be either firm or soft. In time the horse's confidence with water will grow as well as his confidence and trust in his rider.

Right from the earliest age I always try to walk my young horses through puddles and any other water I can find where I know there is a solid bottom. If the

The first step in overcoming the horse's natural inhibitions about water. Walk the horse into the water and jump from the water to dry land before trying to jump in for the first time

young horse has always been through water and not had a bad experience either in deep water or in boggy ground in water, jumping into water will not seem such an unnatural thing to do.

I remember being eliminated at the water at my first Pony Club Area Trial, and Great Ovation's first novice horse trial finishing in a similar vein. In both cases my preparation had been somewhat lacking and both horses later became good water jumpers. Familiarity and repetition were the secret: riding them through water every day wherever I could find it.

Some people believe that swimming a horse helps its confidence in water. There is a certain logic to that, although I have never been able to substantiate it. Undoubtedly, though, horses do enjoy the sea after the initial excitement of going through the waves. It always pays to give a young horse a lead the first time you go into the sea because it would be a disaster if you tried to get him in and failed.

Making sure that you win if you are going to make an issue of something is a vital ingredient in training any horse: it applies to many, many questions, not just water. If ever a horse thinks he can get away with something, it will always be a problem. Therefore only take issue with him at a time and a place when you know you can win.

When training a horse to jump into water I always use shallow water with a firm bottom and preferably a flat approach, and a piece of water that the horse is already familiar with and is quite happy to walk, trot or canter through. It is simplest to start with two show jump stands and a cross-pole. I begin with the cross-pole 18ft back from the water's edge, then reduce the distance 3ft at a time to 15ft, 12ft, 9ft and then put it right on the water's edge so that the horse has to land directly into the water.

It may be a painstaking process, but it is much better to proceed that way, keeping everyone's confidence high, than try to rush it and cause an upset. One bad jump that frightens the horse can undo months and months of hard work and sometimes the horse's confidence never returns.

I believe it is dangerous to have your cross-pole less than 9ft from the water's edge. At 9ft the horse has time to land on grass before going into the water. If there is less than 9ft the horse will still try to land on the grass before going into the water, but the shorter the distance, the closer his feet will land to the back of the fence and the more chance there is of his hitting the fence with his hindlegs or of his body overtaking his front legs before he gets all his feet on the ground.

Another way of tackling the problem is to start by trotting through the water and jumping out over your cross-pole. Once the horse is confident that way about, simply reverse the process. So much depends on the temperament and character of each individual horse and how you as the rider feel he will cope the best. Either way, start with the cross-pole and slowly make it bigger; and always stop while the horse is still jumping confidently and within himself and before he starts to get tired.

When using a straight show jump rail for cross-country schooling I always put two rails very close together so that they resemble a larger pole of the type that would be found on a cross-country fence; and of course I always have a ground line in order to be as kind as possible to the horse.

In time you will be able to progress to repeating a similar process but with a bit of a drop into water, say off a small step. Go up and down the step into the water to start with, then use a cross-rail, then straight rails on the edge of the step. Confidence is so important with water that if I have any doubts or worries with a horse, even an international horse, a confidence-building play in and out of water is not merely a nicety, it is an essential.

Ditches

Ditches cause a disproportionate amount of trouble to horses. They are the simplest of all fences to jump provided the horse does not get frightened and lose his confidence.

When you think about it, a horse would clear most ditches with one galloping stride, so what goes wrong? Once a horse becomes a little uncertain about a ditch, he slows up, loses momentum, his head goes down and he loses balance as he looks at the ditch; at the same time his hindlegs trail out behind him so that he also loses his power and impulsion. Jumping the hole in the ground then becomes very difficult so, if he does go, he lands on all fours or in the face of the bank or leaves his hindlegs in the ditch and the rider hits the back of the saddle and the whole thing becomes an uncomfortable experience. Things go

from bad to worse the next time, and worse still if there is a fence involved.

I always start just with the drainage ditches on the verge of the road, again taking every opportunity with the young horse to trot or hop over as many *small* ditches as I can find. I take particular care never to attempt in the early days anything too deep or too wide. To start with it is much better if a ditch can be jumped or even walked through from a standstill if necessary. I also take particular care to avoid ditches with a downhill approach or sloping take-offs and landings. A sloping take-off makes it more difficult for a horse to keep his balance and a sloping landing punishes the horse if he fails to make the top.

Once a horse is jumping backwards and forwards across a ditch easily and happily, that is, with one constant, free-flowing motion and without any pause, hesitation or dwelling before take-off, I would once again introduce my show jump poles, to start with very small and diagonally across the ditch, with the stands as close to the ditch as possible.

The fence could then be raised, using two rails and jumped either way. Both stands can then be put on the one side of the ditch to create the open ditch or ditch-away type of fence. Again, the secret is always to stop before the fence becomes too big or the horse too tired and while he is still confident and enjoying jumping.

Once the horse has no inhibitions about the ditch, trakehners and open ditches are the easiest of all cross-country obstacles to jump. An open ditch is no more than a triple bar without the middle rail. It is the easiest show jump to jump and the easiest cross-country fence provided it is ridden like the triple bar in the show jumping. You need enough pace to jump the spread, you must not have a stand-off and it does not matter how close you get to the bottom rail or, in the case of a ditch, the take-off rail.

Similarly, a trakehner is the same as a hog's back, the easiest of all profiles to jump. The ditch away is just a rider frightener. If you jump the rail cleanly you will clear the ditch. Horses have a great sense of self-preservation and they are certainly not going to land in a ditch if they can possibly help it.

Riders should always remember that the confident horse looks at the top of what he is jumping and does not have time to look down into the ditch. It is only the horse who bottles out some way back because of his previous experiences who applies the brakes and then looks down at the gaping hole to confirm his worst suspicions.

Coffins

The same principle applies when teaching a horse to jump a coffin. Go backwards and forwards over a nice simple ditch to start with. Then add a cross-pole 18ft beyond the ditch and jump it both ways before adding a second cross-pole 18ft the other side of the ditch. The rails should never come closer than 18ft for the novice horse unless the fence is very, very small. This is so that the novice has plenty of time to land and take a stride that will bring him to his take-off point in front of the ditch.

The distance between the rail and the ditch can come down to 15ft for intermediate horses and 9–12ft for advanced horses, but again when schooling keep the rails small, and never closer than 9ft to the ditch.

On the other side, between the ditch and the rail, the distance needs to be 18ft for novices or 9–12ft for intermediate and advanced horses: that is, a stride for the novices and a bounce for the others. A distance of 15ft should never be used as that is neither one thing nor the other.

The author practising at a coffin suitable for an intermediate horse, with a stride in and a bounce out (a novice horse needs room to take a stride after the ditch). Note how he has maintained his balance throughout while at the same time keeping the horse in front of his leg. Note also the collapse of the hip for the acceleration away from the fence

Banks/Steps

As with everything else, a horse needs to be introduced to banks and steps over a single very small step. I have always found it easier to start by coming down the step first and, having achieved that, then to tackle the upward version. This is because you can always come down from a standstill but the upward journey requires maintenance of a certain degree of power and momentum.

When going up steps the rider has a little work to do in order to stay in balance. If the rider gets in front of the movement, the horse can catch a toe and trip or stumble on top of the bank. It is fatal to get in front of the movement going down a step for if a horse pecks on landing, it usually has disastrous consequences for the rider, who is not in any position to help retrieve the situation. Similarly, if the rider's bottom hits the back of the saddle because he is behind the movement on the way up a step, the horse normally gets punished: with the rider's weight suddenly hitting the saddle, he cannot get his hindlegs up high enough, which is when he leaves a leg behind or hits it against the front of the bank.

Drops

Drops are more of a rider problem than a horse problem. If the horse jumps on and off a bank, then he is unlikely to be frightened of drops.

The problems arise on the approach, when it is crucial for the rider to keep the horse balanced. First practise balancing the horse when riding up and down hills. Going up a hill is easier. The rider must keep his weight far enough forward so as not to hit the back of the saddle. He should still be vertical in relation to level ground, but to retain this position he will have to be nearer to the horse's ears than usual.

Going downhill the rider must sit up more, with his body further away from the horse's ears and the reins a little longer in order to keep that same balance relative to level ground. In order to keep in balance in relation to the horse he will have to sit back, but not so far that the weight falls on to the seat bones. The rider's weight should remain going down through the knees on to the balls of the feet and inevitably the foot will be closer to the horse's shoulder.

If the horse stops at a drop, it is usually the fault of the rider, who has kept the handbrake on because he

is nervous about launching out into space.

As long as the horse is in a rhythm, balanced and going forward you will be able to take off close to the fence and he will have time to see what is expected of him. If the horse takes off a long way back, he will make a big jump, landing a long way out the other side, which is also usually a long way down. If the horse takes off closer, he will have more time to look at the fence, weigh up what is required of him and throw a sensible jump rather than launching himself into space.

Whatever the jump, though, the rider should stay in balance. The bigger the jump, the steeper the descent, the more the rider has to sit up and slip the reins and the further forward the lower leg has to come to support the upper body so that the rider can help the horse on landing. Supporting the upper body with the lower leg and slipping the reins are not just refinements, they are essential skills to be mastered if a rider is to enjoy any sort of life expectancy over cross-country fences.

Corners

Corners are dreaded by many riders but really there is no need as it is so simple to train a horse to be very good at jumping them. All you need is a 40-gallon drum or a dustbin, two stands and five poles. You set the corner up at a very narrow angle with the apex on the drum and the stands equidistant from the centre pole as in the diagram.

The principle of jumping any corner is that you bisect the angle of the two rails and jump that imaginary line at right angles. Any corner then becomes simply a question of jumping a small oxer. The secret is not to cheat when the fence is very small. Yes, you can start off a little nearer the centre than normal to start with, but not dead centre. This is simply a question of riding a small oxer on a line. To do this the horse has to be going forward and you have to be holding him on the line with your hands. If you see a long one and surrender the front end, the horse is free to go wherever he likes and it is normally easier for him not to jump the fence.

Conversely, you must not be hooking and pulling so much that the horse does not know whether it is the accelerator or the handbrake that you are really applying. Whatever your inhibitions, you have to apply the basic principles of keeping your leg on for power, keeping the horse balanced for rhythm and waiting for the fence and the stride to come to you.

I like using striped show jump poles for this exercise as it helps me identify my line easily. Then once the horse is jumping confidently over the very narrow corner, I keep widening the stands by an equal amount from the centre pole and keep coming down to the corner on the same line. The horse knows what he has to do and jumps the corner quite readily, even when it gets quite wide, provided the rider keeps his nerve and keeps coming to the fence the same way. It is quite easy to get the young horse jumping corners at 80°–90° and the advanced horse out to 120°. It does wonders for the morale and confidence of the rider, while at the same time being a very good training exercise for the horse.

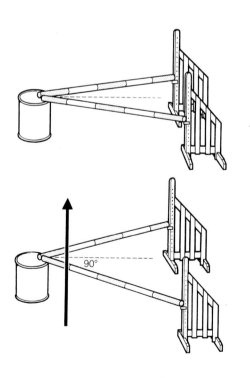

To jump a corner you must jump the imaginery line that bisects the angle at right angles

Problems

Sooner or later a horse is going to stop or glance off with you across country. If he does not, you are possibly going all the long routes and not trying! If a horse stops, always ask youself three questions: (1) Did I give the horse a chance to jump the fence or was it my fault that he stopped? (2) Was the horse frightened of the fence, did he lack the confidence to jump it or did he not understand what he was supposed to be doing? (3) Was he being naughty? If the reason was (1), it was the rider's fault and the horse should be comforted, not chastised. If it was (2), again it was the rider's fault for overfacing the horse or not preparing him well enough for the competition. As soon as possible you need to find a similar obstacle in miniature and build up the horse's confidence once again. If it was (3), some discipline might be necessary. But if the horse is not enjoying the sport, no amount of discipline will prevent him from stopping and maybe he should be in a different line of business.

RIDING A LINE

Increasingly in horse trials more and more accuracy is being asked of horse and rider. This is not going to go away, as falls become more unacceptable and more emphasis is put on the skill of the rider, so we might as well start getting good at it.

Haymaking and harvest time always used to be my favourite time of year as a boy. Jumping a single bale sideways on was quite easy, two high was more difficult and three high a problem! These days I tend to use one half of a show jump filler or upturned plastic dustbins. The show jump filler is easy, three dustbins side by side quite easy, two more difficult and to canter backwards and forwards over a single dustbin in the middle of a field is a problem – but quite possible and something I do quite regularly.

It is an exercise in accurate riding but also in training the horse to jump where he is pointed. To help the horse with the single dustbin I normally start with V rails resting on it. When the horse is jumping happily both ways over that I then lay the V on the ground beside the dustbin and finally take the rails away altogether.

Providing the rider remembers his golden rules it is surprising how quickly the horse becomes quite good at this, and how simple riding a line then seems on the cross-country course.

JUMPING THE CROSS-COUNTRY FENCE

The actual jumping of the cross-country fences differs very little from show jumping. Keeping the horse going forward, balanced and in the resulting rhythm, and waiting for the stride to come are all now even more important because your safety depends on them. The bottom line is that when going across country you jump the fences as fast as you safely can, with the emphasis on safety. Safety comes from balance and rhythm; therefore you have to slow down to the speed at which you can have sufficient balance in order to jump each particular fence.

If you are coming downhill to an upright gate, you need more balance and therefore will have to go more slowly than if you are going uphill to a triple bar; but balance you must have and you must allow yourself enough time before the obstacle to balance the horse up for the fence. If you are not a believer in this theory, be sure to dial for the ambulance before you set out because it will only be a matter of time before you require its services.

It does not matter how fast you go between the fences, though conditions underfoot will often dictate your speed. When approaching a cross-country fence you slow down to the speed at which you can have the horse sufficiently balanced for the obstacle in question, remembering always that balance comes from the leg to the hand. This is a very difficult but vital thing to remember, particularly on a hard-pull-

ing horse and when a horse is getting tired at the end of the course and leaning heavily on the hand. You then have to make yourself keep the leg on to keep the power up and the horse going forward, keep the horse's head up to get him balanced and wait for the stride and the fence to come.

If you feel the revs dying on you or the horse starting to back off, you have no choice other than to go for an extra stride. That is the only way in which you can keep the horse on his feet and any sort of rhythm going. If you start to push and shove, you will lose both power and balance, with the inevitable consequences.

In the heat of competition every now and again riders inevitably end up going on a long stride and having a stand-off. When you do go on that long one you have to give it full power with the leg and lift the horse off the ground with your hand to give him the necessary support, the balance having been lost. You will often hear the top riders saying, 'I'm afraid I saw a bit of a long one going into so and so.' 'I'm afraid' are the operative words. For certain, at the next fence they would put all their ducks back in a row and come to it with balance and rhythm. That way they keep credit in the 'bank' – which is why they are the top riders.

In America recently I heard it put very succinctly. Every time you take off from a good spot you put a dollar in the bank as you help build up the horse's confidence. Every time you see a long one or have a stand-off you take five dollars out as you are sapping the horse's confidence and relying on his bravery to get you to the other side. Are you, I wonder, in credit or overdrawn?

7

FITNESS

Event horses are special athletes: athletes who need the power and suppleness of the gymnast, the speed of a middle-distance runner, the bravery of a rugby forward, the nimbleness of a fencer and the stamina of the marathon runner. As with all athletes, fitness is of paramount importance. Too much work and not enough fitness result in those all-too-common injuries that plague athletes the world over.

There is a saying about making your own luck, and for certain every successful athlete can look back at times when they were favoured by good fortune. For certain also every athlete has blamed bad luck when things have not gone according to plan, whereas, if they were strictly honest with themselves, the setback could have been avoided with better preparation.

I have been very lucky in my lifetime. I have had the opportunity to compete on a number of top-class horses: Rock On, Chicago, Great Ovation, Columbus, Persian Holiday, Lincoln and Cartier. Of those seven, only two, Chicago and Columbus, were truly world-class – and this in a career of twenty-two years of international competition. Statistically my own experience shows that I was lucky enough to find a top-class horse once every three years and a world-beater once every eleven. I hope this helps to illustrate just how important it is to look after your good horse when you find one, and just how important it is to leave no stone unturned in your preparation. The horse must be fit enough to do the work you are asking of him and you must not ask too much too often.

That way you can keep a fit, healthy, happy horse who will last you through many years of competition.

WALKING

I have always believed that all fitness work should start at the walk and on the roads. I believe there is no substitute for the long slow process of gradually toning up the muscles and tendons which have become slack through the weeks of inactivity while the horse has been on holiday. Even if a horse has only had a three-week rest I would still give him a week on the roads before starting to do any sort of training. Individual horses differ so much and at the end of the day they all need individual programmes, but if pressed I would say that as a rule of thumb a horse needs a week's walking on the roads for every three weeks that he has been on holiday.

When preparing a horse for a three-day event I build up the walking exercises until he is doing two hours a day. For the younger horses, with a one-day event programme in mind, an hour a day would suffice, but longer would still be better.

How quickly can we get to two hours a day is the immediate question. Again it is difficult to give a definite answer as so much depends on the individual horse and the terrain over which you are riding. Remember, though, that this is an exercise in toning and hardening. You do not want to sweat off all the condition which you have worked so hard to put on. There is plenty of time for that later on. If the horse is sweating a lot or getting tired and lethargic, you are probably doing too much. If you are in flat country, you can go further more quickly than if you live in the hills. You cannot get a horse fit by following a set of instructions in a textbook. The book can only be a guide; you the rider must look at and feel what is happening underneath you and adapt your programme accordingly.

TROTTING

In the same way that you systematically extended the length of the walking exercise, trotting too should have a logical progression. A short trot and then a walk, a longer trot and then a walk and so on.

Where possible I always like to trot where there is some better going, uphill if possible. If I am on the roads I only ever trot uphill and then only slowly. That way the hack often dictates where and when I trot, but not to the extent that I trot further or up a steeper hill than I think the horse is ready for.

I am lucky at Gatcombe in that I am surrounded by hills. Here the rule of thumb is very easy: trot up the hills, walk down them and only trot in between if there is some good footing. Apart from galloping days and the rest day, I would expect horses preparing for a three-day event to work up to doing two hours a day on the hills after they have done their dressage or jumping schooling. I would obviously endeavour to increase the length, steepness and frequency of the hills as the horse becomes fitter.

Those horses doing a two-star event with its slower speeds and shorter distances could possibly get by with, say, one and a half hours a day and, similarly, for a one-star event, one hour a day. But once again it is the work that the horse does while he is out and how he is feeling on the day that should dictate the length of work, rather than the watch or the textbook.

CANTERING AND GALLOPING

Questions I am always being asked are how far should I gallop, how often and how fast? The blunt truth is that you should let the horse tell you. He should always want to go a bit faster and a bit further than you are allowing.

For years I used to gallop round and round fields on marginal going not really knowing what I was doing and boring my horse half to death. The man who changed all that for me was Fred Winter, at a time when he was so far ahead as the leading National Hunt trainer that nobody really knew who was second.

The first thing he said that hit home was that he never galloped any of his horses for more than a mile and a half, even ones destined for the Grand National or the Cheltenham Gold Cup. So much for me going round and round my field for twenty minutes! The second thing he said was that you cannot get a horse fitter than fit. How often had I tried to go that little bit faster for that little bit further.

These days, with the advanced horses destined for a CCI, I grasp the nettle and box them to racehorse gallops, in spite of all the facilities I have at Gatcombe. Once there I go up the gallop against the collar, uphill, for six furlongs at half pace. When I say half pace I am really saying that I am going at a speed where the horse is working comfortably well within himself, in the 525-500 metres per minute area. Then I walk down the gallop, turn and go a mile and a quarter to the top, travelling a little bit faster than the first time, in the region of 570-600 mpm. If at any stage I feel the horse starting to come off the bridle I slow up. Maybe on the first occasion I am only able to do six furlongs, and the second as well. But as the weeks pass the horse will be able to go further, faster, the second time up.

Some horses pull harder than others. The hard pullers I would always gallop in front or by themselves. Those with a more lethargic nature benefit from going up with another horse, but again never off the bridle.

What is the object of galloping? Yes, to exercise and stretch the galloping muscles; but more importantly, to make the horse have a 'blow'. That is, while he is galloping, to get him to take that extra deep breath which opens the lungs right out. If I can achieve that both times up the gallop and keep the

Fast work, designed to exercise the muscles and give the horses a 'blow'. The more lethargic horse benefits from galloping 'up-sides'

horse on the bridle all the way, he will have done some really good work. If he only has a blow the once, especially as he becomes fitter, it would not worry me. I have after all achieved my main reason for going for a gallop.

Why do I go to so much trouble, putting the horses in a lorry and driving an hour to the gallops? It is quite simple: on the racehorse gallops I can do the maximum amount of work on good footing for the minimum amount of mileage and wear and tear on the horse's legs. I would rather take that trouble and complete my work against the collar over a total distance of two miles than have to gallop five miles on moderate footing somewhere else in order to do the same amount of work. I discovered much too late in life how important it is not to leave any stone unturned and just how important it is to put the least amount of pressure, wear and tear on a horse's limbs in training in order to have the benefit of the longest possible competitive span.

PIPE OPENER

From my own experiences as an athlete, I know how easy it is to arrive at a competition or match leg-weary, having overtrained. Therefore, before the cross-country of a three-day event I would keep the horse off the hills for a full seven days, just hack him out instead, and simply give him a pipe opener on the Tuesday before going across country on the Saturday.

A 'pipe opener' is exactly what it says it is: a gallop simply to open out the airways. Often just a nice three-quarter pace for six or eight furlongs is enough to get the horse to take that all-important deep breath to open out his lungs. However, if one trip is not enough, he will undoubtedly have a blow second time up.

If you work a horse for some time on one particular gallop, you will get a feel of how far and how fast you have to go to make the horse have a blow. I have found that horses nearly always do it at the same place.

HILLWORK

Increasingly I have found myself doing more and more of my fittening work on the hills. I am lucky enough to have many hills round about and so four days a week the horses are out there, initially walking, then trotting up the hills. I am quite happy once they have started trotting for them really to work on the hills. Often they will sweat and breathe heavily, recover between hills and then go again.

It is a form of interval training in a way, but how much less wear and tear we do exercising on the hills at the trot than going round and round at the canter! I believe hills are where I really get my horses fit. If I did not have any on my doorstep, I would box the horses to an area where there are hills at least twice a week. I believe the hillwork to be just as important as the galloping and I am equally convinced that the hills and galloping complement each other, eventually giving you the fitness you need to take you to injury-free success at the three-day event.

I have often wondered what I would do if I lived in a very flat country miles from the nearest hills. The more I have thought about it the more perplexed I have become. I suppose you would have to resort to big-time interval training. I have never indulged in interval training myself and therefore do not feel qualified to set down a doctrine. I have, however, watched many riders practise it and I have always had great concern for all the wear and tear involved on the horse's legs.

That brings me to the conclusion that if I were living in a very flat area, I would have to believe that I was putting myself at an intolerable disadvantage compared to my peers. I appreciate that the alternative could be both expensive and unpalatable in that the final preparations may have to be done away from home where the facilities are better.

LEVEL OF FITNESS

How do you tell how fit your horse is? That is something I find almost impossible to quantify in words and it is an area where there is no substitute for experience. I find, though, that the time taken until the horse has completely recovered after a good piece of work as good a guide as any. If the horse, having had a good blow, is totally recovered – that is, there is no visible sign of movement in either nostrils or flanks when the horse is breathing – in twelve minutes, he is pretty fit. If he takes longer than twelve minutes then there is still room for improvement.

Another guide is the rate of breathing. If a horse is taking slow deep breaths, he is much fitter than the horse taking sharp, short breaths.

I look at the condition of the horse, too. When you look at the horse's side you should be able to see the prominent muscle over the ribs. When you run your hand along the horse's side his skin should move in multiple little ripples in front of your fingers.

Some people employ more sophisticated methods, using heart-rate monitors and other high-tech devices. I am sure these things can help. I am equally sure they should only be a guide and that what you feel ultimately determines the amount of work you do. I have always preferred to trust in what I am feeling under me and to take note of the length of the horse's recovery period. However, I do have a blood sample taken during the first month of training and again six or eight weeks later to make sure that the horse's blood profile is in order. Obviously if there is a problem or I am in any way concerned during training, I would have another taken whenever necessary to make sure all is in order.

Similarly, if I had any worries about a horse's wind, I would not hesitate to call the vet out to have a look with an endoscope.

COMPETITIONS

Over the years I have found it almost impossible to get a horse fit for a three-day event with just gallops and work at home. A one-day event will 'bring the horse on' no end. I am always amazed at how much fitter horses are after they have had a run.

I have found that three runs before a three-day event is ideal from a fitness point of view. It may be that you want to do extra outings from an educational or training standpoint, but fitness-wise three outings should bring the horse pretty much to a peak.

When running him in competitions it is important to select courses where the going is good and the fences well built. Some events have relatively easy courses, others are very difficult, and care should be taken that the horse's first outings are over the former. For me these Novice one-day events are part of the educational process and not ends in themselves. I take every precaution not to put the young horse at risk, when he might injure himself or lose his confidence. If I get to an event and do not like the

Hillwork is just as important as galloping, and the two complement each other

FITNESS PROGRAMME

Week					Advanced	Intermediate	Novice
1	Walk						
2							
3							
4							
5		Trot					
6				Dressage training			
7					Jumping training	Dressage show ⟶	
8			Gallop			Jumping show ⟶	
9						Dressage/ jumping show ⟶	
10						HT (OI/A)	HT (I)	HT (N)
11						?Dressage/ jumping show ⟶	HT (N)
12						HT (A)	HT (I)	?Dressage/ jumping show
13						?Dressage/ jumping show ⟶	HT (N)
14						HT (A)	HT (I)	HT (N)
15								
16						CCI★★★★/ CCI★★★	CCI★★	CCI★★

NB This programme can obviously be considerably condensed if the horse has only had a short break and has retained a good level of fitness.

FITNESS PROGRAMME

Typical Week

	Training Week	*Prior to a One-day Event*	*Post One-day Event*
Mon	Dressage and hills	Dressage and hills	Rest
Tues	Gallop	Gallop	Walk out
Wed	Dressage and hills	Dressage and hills	Light dressage and light hills/hack
Thurs	Show jumping and hills	Show jumping and hills	Dressage and hills
Fri	Gallop	Gallop (pipe opener)	Gallop
Sat	Dressage and hack	Dressage and hack	Dressage and hack
Sun	Rest or dressage/show jumping show	One-day event	Rest or dressage/show jumping show

NB Gallop 2 × per week except after one-day event.
   Short gallop/pipe opener last gallop before one-day event.
   No hills the day before a competition.

course or the going, I often do just the dressage and the show jumping, or pull up on the cross-country before I come to the bad going or a bad fence. This never gets a round of applause from the organisers but if you go and thank them before you leave and explain your horse's problem, they will normally welcome you back the following year.

We are lucky in England that there are so many horse trials. Young horses can be taken to Novice events until they are going confidently and until they are doing so I avoid upgrading by going slowly across country. It is no use trying to tackle Intermediate courses before a horse is completely happy over a Novice course. The problems usually occur with horses who do good dressage and are therefore likely to upgrade too quickly. With such horses I often have to go round the cross-country at half speed in order to accumulate time faults and avoid winning prizes. I can then keep them in Novice events until they are confident enough to take on Intermediate courses.

I do not like doing a three-day event with a six-year-old as it puts unnecessary mileage on the clock. I prefer to run him in Novice horse trials and eventually upgrade to Intermediate one-day events when the horse is ready. I usually enter an event every weekend but rarely run one horse every weekend. I select carefully according to the going, the fences and what he did the previous week. I might run a horse two weekends running, but never four, though I will occasionally do a maximum three events a month. These days, with the problems of balloting, the choice is perhaps not as big as it used to be. If you eventually get your run at a less suitable location, there is no alternative but to jump around slowly and safely.

For a horse's first Intermediate or Advanced I take care to choose a good course and good going, as it is quite a step up in terms of the size of the fences and the speed required. Slippery going in particular should be avoided with young horses, particularly when they first upgrade.

CROSS-COUNTRY SCHOOLING

I am not a great advocate of cross-country schooling, but if I *am* going to gallop about and jump a lot of fences, I would try to do it on a gallop day and treat it in the same way. All too often cross-country schooling is for the benefit of the rider's confidence and not the horse's education. So many people make the mistake of trying to school at the level at which they are competing instead of one level down. In cold blood and at half or threequarter pace it is very difficult to school over 'big' fences without frightening the horse and negating the whole effect of the school.

SWIMMING

Swimming is an aid to general fitness but no substitute for work on the gallops. Over the years I have swum my horses a lot, but only when the gallops have been frozen or the horse has had a temporary setback such as a bruised foot.

A number of people have tried to go straight from the swimming pool to a competition. In my experience this has always ended in tears. If the horse will not stand his last piece or two of work on the gallops, for certain he will not stand the rigours of a competition.

SPEEDS

When talking about galloping I have deliberately not talked about going so many metres per minute for so many furlongs in week one and week two and so on, because how the individual horse feels, the footing and the gradient will all affect how far and how fast you go.

Having said that, being able to judge how fast you are going on a particular horse is an essential skill for the horse trials rider. Many is the competition that has been lost by the rider going too fast or too slowly on the steeplechase or by starting out too fast or two slowly on the cross-country.

You must be able to judge when you are going 500, 600 or 700 metres per minute. It is an interesting exercise to peg out the distances and then time yourself at a regular pace between the pegs. If you have to slow down or accelerate towards the end you are fooling no one but yourself.

8

RIDING CROSS-COUNTRY FENCES

The exhilaration of galloping at speed over cross-country fences is the nectar of horse trials. It is what makes all the trials and tribulations worthwhile. To ride well, as near the limit but as safely as possible, is what it is all about. If it is not done well, crossing the country can be downright frightening and dangerous.

THE BALANCED, FORWARD APPROACH

Riding cross-country fences well all comes down to the rider being able to remain balanced, while at the same time having the horse going forward at the optimum speed and with sufficient balance to jump the fence in question.

I am a great believer in the rider staying balanced during the approach to the fence, through take-off to the top of the fence and only coming behind the movement on the descent, ready for touchdown. For the vast majority of fences jumped, this is the ideal and one which is not that difficult to attain. Coming behind the movement on landing is one of the relatively few areas where cross-country riding differs from show jumping, where you land with the movement of the horse.

There is a school of thought which believes that the rider should sit down and drive his horse at every cross-country fence. This I have never found to be necessary and I believe that it often creates the wrong idea about cross-country riding. When you are approaching a cross-country fence with sufficient pace and balance, why sit in the saddle, get behind the movement of the horse, drive him at the fence and upset the balance, when it is much simpler just to keep him on his feet and wait for the stride and the fence to come to you?

In moments of stress, when suddenly the revs start to drop, and the power and balance are failing fast, it is another matter. Then you do need to come down to the saddle and use everything at your disposal – legs, whip, weight, voice, hands and anything else you can think of – to maintain as much power and momentum as possible in order somehow to get to the other side. Once the niceties have gone out of the window, a little time lost on landing and moving away from the fence are of only minor importance. The one thing on your mind is how to get the horse to the other side of the fence, keeping your fingers crossed that he does not tip over in the process.

There will be a number of people on novice or younger horses who will say they find it easier to sit down and push their horses to the fences. To them I would put the following three questions: Is the horse going forward, is he balanced and are they waiting for the fence and stride to come? In all probability they need go no farther than question one. For if the horse is not going forward, in front of the leg, up to the hand, if he does not have the desire to go forward and is not saying, 'Come on, mum, let's go and jump this fence', or however you like to think of it, there suddenly arises the need to generate more power:

hence the desire to sit down and push. For me, that has always been the frightening bit of cross-country riding. I have no desire to ride cross-country fences on a horse who is under-powered and not going forward. I would prefer to go back to the drawing board and create what I need at home, or in the show jumping ring, before setting sail at fixed timber. I prefer to leave the odd moments when I am reduced to going on a wing and a prayer to the self-inflicted occasions of extreme stress in a competition, when I have been going too fast, turned too tight or left my setting-up process too late.

As with all jumping, the fence itself is the comparatively easy part, providing the set-up has been good. As always, the first thing is to ensure that you keep your leg on in order to keep the horse going forward. If the horse is going flat out, he is not going forward, because when he is at maximum mph he cannot have the desire to go faster. Therefore, you have to keep the leg on and slow down to the speed at which you can have him sufficiently balanced for the type of fence you are jumping.

With the leg maintaining the mph you require, it is then only a case of balancing the horse up. Remember always that the balancing process comes from the leg to the hand and that it is a particularly difficult one on a hard-pulling horse or on a horse who is starting to tire. In front of every fence I picture the place where I am going to put my leg on and balance the horse up. Power plus balance gives you rhythm. When you have rhythm at the pace you need it is simply a question of maintaining it, waiting until the fence and the stride come to you, and bingo, the horse has every chance to jump the fence.

SLIPPING THE REINS

Having stayed in balance throughout the approach and take-off, the rider must now be prepared to come behind the movement of the horse for landing. This necessitates the conscious effort of pushing the foot forward slightly, while at the same time sitting up a little more quickly and going back a little further than normal, slipping the reins if necessary. Then, in the first stride after landing, the rider can collapse the hips to get the weight forward again up over the knees, while at the same time putting hand over hand over hand to shorten the reins, pick the horse up and

Jumping a fence off a bank; just like jumping any other drop fence. Note the good lower leg position and the slipping of the reins, and that the rider has already started to turn the horse to the right

move him away from the fence.

Slipping the reins is not old-fashioned or something only the British indulge in. It is an essential skill for the cross-country rider. The steeper and longer the descent to touchdown, the greater the requirement to open the fingers and allow the reins to 'slip' through if the rider is not to be pulled forward and out of balance. Having sat up and slipped the reins, it is then easy to close the fingers and give the horse the support he needs on landing.

It is essential to use reins which will slip through your fingers. Web reins, fitted with leather 'stops' are a disaster because when you try to slip them the stop either catches on your finger and pulls you forward, or it catches on your finger and the rein jumps out of your hand. I have always used 'rubber' reins across country. The top riders become very quick at gathering their reins together on landing. Sometimes things might not go to plan and you find yourself left with your reins a little long at the next fence, if it comes up very quickly. The result may not be pretty but it is still infinitely preferable to being pulled forward out of balance and in front of the movement.

On any cross-country course there are always a number of fences where time is of secondary importance and the absolutely vital thing is to be going forward at the right speed and with enough balance and power when you arrive at the fence. The technical fences such as coffins, sunken roads, quarries, light into dark, water, corners, combinations and any fence requiring an accurate line all come into this category. For these fences it is sometimes necessary to start your set-up 100, 200 or 500 yards before the fence, or sometimes even before the previous fence, according to the rideability of your particular horse.

COFFIN

In any fence analysis the coffin is always one of the most influential fences on the course. The most difficult version found at the highest level of the sport is when the first set of rails is on the edge of a bank and the ditch is only 9ft away in a hollow. If the ground slopes down steeply towards the ditch, creating a drop after the first rail, you have the ultimate coffin question, especially when there is a wide ditch and another rail just 9ft or 12ft away on the other side of the ditch.

To jump a coffin the horse must be going forward in the take-off stride and with as much power as possible at as slow a speed as possible. This obviously varies from horse to horse according to his individual athleticism and level of training. 'The coffin canter' is an expression often used by riders. It means maintaining the horse's desire to go forward, at as slow, bouncy and powerful a canter as you can possibly muster.

The reason for this type of canter is to give the horse as much power as possible to jump the first element – preferably with a little bit in reserve in case the ditch takes him by surprise – while at the same time allowing him as much time as possible to see what he has to jump and where he can put his feet to land.

If the rider gets it right and comes in a good rhythm to a deep spot in front of the first element, the horse has plenty of time to weigh up the situation, pop the rail, stay on his feet, progress to the ditch and then to the final element. On the other hand, if the rider is going too fast, with not enough balance, or has a stand-off, the trajectory of the jump will take the horse much too close to the ditch or even into it. In that case the only options open to the horse are to stop altogether or to drop his hindlegs on the fence to steady himself up before the ditch. The bottom line though is that in those all-important last two strides, right or wrong, too slow or too fast, the rider has to be 110 per cent committed to jumping the fence. If the rider is still saying 'whoa' or 'steady' when he gets to the fence, nine times out of ten the horse will do as requested and stop.

The aim of the rider at all cross-country fences, and most certainly the technical ones, should be to keep the horse going forward, balanced and on his feet at all times. That means not being in a hurry and rushing the horse at the fence but keeping hold of his mouth in order to give him the support he needs to stay balanced. People so often ask me how many strides a horse will put in at a cross-country fence. In most cases my answer is that it does not matter. Allow the horse to do what he wants, just keep him balanced and going forward and he will handle the problem in the way he sees as the best.

How a distance rides in a coffin depends greatly on the ground. The effects of undulating or sloping ground can give an infinite number of variations. I always try to picture where the horse will land and to assess where he will arrive to take off over the ditch and over the rail on the way out. This helps me to work out the best speed at which to approach the first element.

There are so many variables that it is difficult to make firm rules. For example, if there is a very wide ditch with a rail just 9ft after it, the coffin should ride well because the horse will tend to land only a short distance from the ditch and bounce out. If, however, it is a narrow ditch, then 9ft to the next rail would be very short; 12ft would be a more sympathetic distance. If the distance is 15ft, then it is a question of knowing your horse: if he is bold and likes standing back, with sufficient pace he will bounce out; if he likes to shuffle and take off close, then provided he is allowed the time, he will take an extra short stride and pop out. However, it is unusual to have a comfortable ride at 15ft coming out of a coffin because it is neither one thing nor the other. On the other hand, at 18ft most horses would take a comfortable short stride.

SUNKEN ROAD

A sunken road presents a very similar question to the coffin. The all-important factor is the distance from the first element to the edge of the sunken road. The shorter distance of 9ft is very much an advanced question whereas 18ft allows the horse to put in a stride and may therefore be only a novice question. Again the important thing is to come to the first element from a strong bouncy canter approach – not too fast but going forward those last two or three strides. The further back the rail is from the edge of the sunken road, the easier it is to jump and the more pace can be used in the approach.

The most difficult distance is when there is only 9ft on which to land. Then the approach must be very

The coffin, always one of the most influential fences on the course. The author on Columbus at Badminton. Note his balance and the way he has the horse 'in front of him'

slow and full of impulsion, identical to that required at the coffin. For many of the distances it is a question of knowing your horse. If it is the dreaded 15ft across the bottom, the free-going horse can bounce it, but the shorter-striding one can pop in and take a shuffly stride before hopping out. Again this is the most difficult distance to ride and what happens at the bottom very often depends on how the horse jumps the rail on the way in. With 18ft most horses take one stride if they are in a balance; those going too quickly or a bit flat often try to bounce.

At all times the rider must concentrate on staying balanced. If he gets in front of the movement, the horse may leave a front leg on the rails on the way in or on the step on the way out of the road; if he gets left behind, the horse may leave a hindleg at either place. Both will result in a stop at the last element, particularly if there is no room for a stride after coming up out of the road.

There are many different ways of tackling a sunken road. Account has to be taken of both the depth of the road and the distances. If there is 12ft to land on and 21ft in the bottom of the road, an advanced horse can approach with a bit of pace on. On the other hand, to land on 12ft would be very short for a novice.

If the horse has to shorten in the bottom of a sunken road, he will jump out less far, so that 9ft to the final element would usually be best. If the momentum can be kept up when jumping down and across the road, 12ft to a rail would suit most horses. Again, how the horse jumps one element will affect the next and all will be affected by how he jumps the first rail.

There are so many variables for so many horses that when I walk the course I always try to imagine how my horse will jump it, where he will land and how he will react, and then plan to adjust my rhythm accordingly.

QUARRY

A quarry is simply a big drop fence. But again, because the horse cannot see until the last moment where he is going to land, the rider must give him time in the final stride to see what has to be done and where there is to put his feet.

This again requires a slow but powerful approach, though often you can have a bit more pace than for a coffin. The important thing is to allow plenty of time for the set-up, because you must have good rhythm in the approach. If the rhythm is lacking, and you cannot come to your deep spot but go off a longish, flat stride, you are in big-time trouble. If the horse is brave enough to launch himself into space, he will be going on a flat trajectory, which means he could touch down a long way out and a frighteningly long way down, with the risk of turning over on landing.

Good rhythm, and moving forward in the last two or three strides to the base of the fence, will allow the horse to look, think, use himself over the fence and jump economically down to the easiest landing place.

Going into a quarry always presents a major rein-slipping exercise for the rider. Failure to slip the reins normally results in a painful, unscheduled dismount!

LIGHT INTO DARK

I never like jumping from bright sunlight into darkness. Knowing where the shadows are going to be is always a very good reason for walking the course, if possible, at the same time of day that you are going to ride it.

In fact, I believe that horses have better eyesight than most of their riders and can adjust to changing light conditions much more quickly that we can. However, because I have never been able to prove my theory, I have always taken particular care with light-into-dark fences and at the very least throttle down to show jumping pace to give the horse time to see exactly what he is being asked to jump, at the same time being sure to keep the power up in case he is taken by surprise.

WATER

Jumping into water is not something that horses would do naturally. Therefore it always requires very positive riding in order to give the horse the confidence he lacks. However, positive riding does not mean pace. Miles per hour are no substitute for technique and it is amazing how quickly horses can stop – often quicker than their riders.

I always try to be at about half speed, or a strong

Big drop fences require a major rein-slipping exercise for the rider so that her balance can be maintained. The maintenance of a strong lower leg position once again is vital in order to give the rider the platform on which to balance herself. Lucinda Green at the Leaf Pit at Burghley

show jumping canter, and then to wind the elastic band up as tightly as I can so that the horse is pulling me into the fence as much as possible. I am never shy about using my voice or the whip down the shoulder as I endeavour to keep the lacky band tight, and to maintain my rhythm all the way to the base of the fence into the water, again always going forward for those last two or three strides.

At the end of the day, though, whether you are right or wrong, too fast or too slow, you must be riding forward through those last few strides to give the horse the confidence he needs. Then there is always the chance that he will come to your rescue. You could easily argue that the same is true for all cross-country fences, and certainly the great cross-country riders are always going forward at every fence. At many fences it is a nicety, but at water it is essential.

Right from my days in the Pony Club I was always taught that it was a cardinal sin to catch the horse in the mouth over a fence. However, I believe that the one exception is when jumping into water, particularly if it is more than 8–9in deep. The rider needs to have a small feel of the teeth to keep the horse's head up while landing into water. That way, the horse lands with his front feet out in front of him, which enables him to keep his balance better when the drag of the water comes into play. If his front legs are too far back on landing, because of the drag of the water, the body can sometimes overtake the legs. The result is invariably an early bath.

Slipping the reins is again very important. Nobody ever quite knows exactly what is going to happen when landing in water. Therefore landing behind the movement in a defensive position is again a necessity, not a nicety.

I have never particularly liked bounces into water, but they do occasionally appear and the solution is always to be a little braver than you feel you would like to be. With the water behind, and probably a drop as well, the distance in a bounce into water always rides longer than it walks because of the horse's backing himself off. Therefore you need to ride a 12ft distance into water as though it were a normal 15ft bounce. At 15ft as many horses as not will put in a little shuffle.

Riders are notoriously bad at riding fences in water and a step up coming out. The reason is that,

When jumping into water the rider should have a feel of the horse's teeth in order to keep the horse's head up and his front feet out in front of him to help him to keep his balance as the drag of the water comes into play

The horse must not be hurried or pushed out of balance when negotiating water

Given the chance, he will always jump out . . .

. . . he does not want to stay in there any longer than necessary, either

Provided he is kept in balance, he will negotiate steps out without difficulty

having got in, they are always in much too much of a hurry to come out. They forget what it was like the last time they went to the beach and tried to run into or out of the sea. In very shallow water there is no problem, but as soon as there is any depth to it, it becomes extremely difficult to run in. Horses have exactly the same problem and therefore they should not be hurried or pushed out of balance. If they are, they invariably leave either a front or back leg, depending on where the rider is sitting at the time. All a rider can do is to maintain what balance and momentum he can, however agonizingly slow that may seem, and wait for the step or fence to come to him. The 'long one' is not an option. Providing the rider keeps hold of the horse's head, given the

chance, a horse will always jump out of water – he does not want to stay in there any longer than necessary, either.

Jumping on to the face of an Irish bank. Note that the rider is gripping with the back of the calf instead of supporting herself on the ball of her foot. Should the horse require assistance to balance himself and change legs on the top of the bank, the rider will find herself in a weak position and will only be able to be of limited assistance

BANKS

Irish Bank

It is very rare to be able to jump clean on to the top of an Irish bank. In fact, I believe that it is much safer if a horse cannot do so. I have never enjoyed jumping a small bank because if you are going too fast, it is very easy for the horse to slide across the top and fall off the other side.

Therefore I always aim to jump on to the face of the bank, prepared all the time to give the horse the support he needs to change legs on the top before jumping off the far side. To do this I normally like to throttle down a little bit from the pace so that the horse has time to do his business on the top and so that the whole thing is not a mad scramble.

Normandy Bank

A Normandy bank is a different kettle of fish. Although the original Normandy bank had a rounded top, with rails off, the modern equivalents all seem to have flat tops, which make life a lot easier. The secret is always to jump up with a view to getting as close as possible to the rails off, so that the horse can jump them like any other drop fence. The Normandy bank at Badminton was 13ft 6in across the top. There you had to go as fast as your horse could lay its legs to the ground in order to get close enough to the rails. Those who failed, and put in a shuffle, normally had a very uncomfortable landing.

Obviously the narrower the distance across the top, the more your pace can be reduced. I hate, though, a low step up to a rail or up on to a bank. A low step completely changes the rules, because at a given pace the lower the step the further on to a bank a horse will jump. It is therefore very easy to over-ride a small step and jump too far on to the bank. Similarly, if you have a very big step up, you need more pace than you may think, otherwise the horse will land very close to the front edge.

Cornish Bank (narrow top, less than 6ft)

I have always followed one golden rule for all table tops, narrow-topped banks and grass-topped fences: ride them to jump them in one and if the horse wants to, he will touch down. That way he has the power to solve the problem in the way he thinks best. Adopting the other alternative – approaching slowly and

Jumping confidently over a fence with a ditch and big drop on the landing side. Note the good lower leg position, which will enable the upper body to come back as the descent begins

107

trying to get the horse to bank the fence – is fine provided you are both on the same wavelength. But if the horse has a mind to jump it in one and is not going fast enough, the result is more often than not catastrophic.

STEP TO A RAIL

A step up with 18ft to a rail is seldom a problem as there is plenty of room for adjustment and for a stride. The problems really start once the distance comes down to the dreaded 15ft. Then it is a question of whether it is a stride or a bounce and much will depend on the size of the step and the individual horse. Similarly, when it comes down to 9ft, that is a very short distance unless there is a big step up.

I have often tried to solve a difficult distance at a step and rail by holding the horse off the step so that he landed on the front edge, thus giving him room to bounce the rail on a short distance or put in a shuffle on a middling distance. Plan A, though, is always to leave the horse in his rhythm as much as possible to allow him to solve the problem his way.

COMBINATION FENCES

I always treat a combination fence as a show jumping exercise. Whatever the distances or related distances between fences, I always revert back to the exercises I have done so often at home. The distance involved dictates the pace and power required, and wherever possible I try to keep the horse travelling in a straight line. Horses jump much better when they can see what is ahead of them and weigh up the problems. If they are suddenly pulled off on to another line, they can sometimes be taken by surprise and make a mistake.

CORNERS

Riding a corner is basically very easy, though it becomes very difficult if you do not obey the simple rules. A corner is all about riding a line, so the first thing is to ensure that you are on the correct one.

To find the line, bisect the angle of the corner and then jump that imaginary line at right angles (see diagram in Chapter 6). To find the line in competition I always pick the spot on the rail where I want to jump

and then, bisecting my imaginary line at right angles, line it up with something on the horizon. The reason for this is that I know that I will be able to see those two reference points when I am competing. If you take reference points at ground level, they invariably become obscured by spectators, a parked car or an ambulance.

As with all line fences, I try to put the horse on the line as early as possible and keep him on it for as long as possible. The longer the horse has to see what he has to do, the better he will jump the fence. Once the horse is on the line, the corner is just like any other oxer, but you have to make particularly sure that you keep the rhythm. If the horse is not going forward, and you have to start pushing, or if he is not balanced, and you start picking at him in front of the fence, he will take the easy option around the outside of the fence. However, if you have rhythm and can simply hold the horse to the fence, corners are not difficult and are great time savers.

BOUNCES AND DOUBLE BOUNCES

Bounces are easily practised at home. Remember, though, that while a 12ft bounce may ride well in a sand arena, it will be very short on a cross-country course unless you throttle right back. Across country a 15ft bounce is a comfortable forward-going distance. As the distance becomes shorter, so you have to go slower and slower in your approach.

Double bounces are always deceptive. Because of the loss of power in the first part, you always have to jump the first element that little bit quicker, that little bit more powerfully than you are really happy about. That way you will have enough residual energy to jump the third element.

OPEN DITCHES AND TRAKEHNERS

I always look forward to the ditches on a cross-country course because once your horse has overcome any initial inhibitions about jumping them, the profile of ditch fences makes them some of the easiest

The trakehner, a fence which can be approached with pace and confidence. The rider has a good lower leg position which would be stronger still if the iron was on the ball of the foot

on the course.

As I pointed out earlier, a trakehner is just like a hog's back and an open ditch like a triple bar without the middle rail. Thought of in those terms, they can be approached with pace and confidence. Take off as close as you can to the edge of the ditch and you are in business.

The trouble is that when walking the course riders have the chance to walk up to a ditch, stare down into the depths of the abyss, gaze across to the rail or brush on the other side and thoroughly put themselves off the idea of jumping it. Then when they come to ride it there is too much hand and not enough leg and they finish up with insufficient power to be able to get close enough to the edge of the ditch for take-off; or else they push and shove the horse at it, throwing away any balance they might have had, and suddenly the more they push, the further they get from where they want to take off and they find themselves looking at a very big fence.

I always go back 20 yards and look at the fence from there. That is how the horse is going to see it when he is travelling at 25mph and it is amazing how much more friendly ditches look from that range.

LANDINGS

I hate to land over any fence into rising ground, nor do I like drop fences on to flat ground. Any fence where the ground runs away on landing is always going to be a good fence for the horse to land over, as touchdown will be soft and there will be very little jar, even over a big drop.

Where you do find drop fences on to flat ground you must be very careful not to go too fast, thereby creating more jar than is necessary. You should aim to achieve as economical a jump as possible. On the odd occasion when you end up landing into rising ground you need a very similar approach, but in addition you must be ready to give the horse much-needed support on landing.

A fence where the ground runs away on landing reduces jar on the horse's legs: note that the pastern and joint are still well up off the ground. Also the lower leg position and the slipping of the reins enable Ian Stark to stay in perfect balance on Murphy Himself as he comes down to the water at Gatcombe

9

COMPETING IN A
ONE-DAY EVENT

The planning of your day at a one-day event really starts from the moment you are able to get your starting times from the secretary of the horse trials in question. The first thing to check is whether you have time to walk the cross-country after your dressage test. If there is an hour-and-a-half window in the day, you will have just about enough time between phases. If your window is less than an hour and a half, you will need help with your horse – and you will have to run. You should always allow an hour to walk a novice course and an hour and a half for an advanced track.

If you end up having to walk the course *before* your dressage test, it is normally going to mean a very early start. You have to work back from the start of your test, taking into account the journey time, walking the course, collecting your number and the riding-in time for the dressage. Often it is better to bite the bullet and travel the evening before, particularly if you can have time to ride on the event site.

THE DRESSAGE PHASE

Riding-in
I believe there is as much skill attached to the riding-in as there is actually to riding the test itself. You really have to keep working to find the formula that best suits your particular horse. In trying to find that formula, you must understand what you are trying to achieve. I have always believed that when riding-in or working-in for a dressage test the main

objective is to get the horse as rideable as possible. Therefore everything I do is designed to encourage him to relax and 'let go' of himself so that I can walk-trot-canter-trot-walk all on a loose rein. Once I can do this, all that remains is to pick the reins up ten minutes before I am due in, do a few movements and I am ready.

I see far too many people trying to do movements when the horse is still more interested in the activities on the other side of the hedge. All this does is to create tension, annoy the horse and put more pressure on the rider as the moment for the test draws ever nearer and the horse becomes more irritated and contrary. Similarly, the day of the competition is not the moment to start trying to improve his half-pass or extended trot. It is all too easy to look across at another competitor and think, 'Oh heck, that's much better than my extension', and immediately go off to try and improve your own. Competition day is about trying to reproduce what you know you can do at home. It is not the right time to expect improvements, particularly with all the prevalent pressures and distractions.

I nearly always start my horses on the lunge so that they have the chance to let off steam and get the bucks and kicks out of their system before I climb on board. It does not matter how much of a seasoned campaigner you are; if the horse is being a real orangutan when you first get on him, it does nothing for your nerves and confidence and it is very difficult to stay totally relaxed and not be a little bit edgy with him.

Once on board, it is a question of starting on the endless routine of half-halts, shoulder-ins, serpentines and figures of eight, in walk, trot and canter, until you can start to get the horse to let go and allow you to ride him. All the time I work towards getting him to stretch and draw the reins through my fingers without losing his balance or changing his rhythm. It is amazing how often even the most high-spirited horses will suddenly say, okay, enough is enough, I am now going to listen. Sometimes it takes a long time. I can well remember riding for three and four hours and often having a horse out two or three times before a test. Sometimes, though, at the one-day events there is not enough time or daylight to do that so you must accept that you are going to have to make the best of a bad job.

One secret is never to be in a hurry or short of time. For certain the first time you ask for too much too soon, because time is running out, it will be the end of a happy combination as almost by definition it creates tension or a resistance. It then takes much longer to get the horse back to where you were before you asked the question.

I have found that some horses are better with a 'cold start'. That is, I go through the whole working-in process, do a few movements and am pretty happy with the state of play. I then take the horse back to the lorry and let him stand in for half an hour or so, bringing him out again ten minutes before the test. The 'switch-off' period in the lorry seems to help the mental relaxation and makes some individuals that much more rideable.

Some horses benefit from being worked several times. They may be started on the lunge, then be ridden, then either be lunged or ridden again, each time with an interval in the stable or lorry before finally coming out to do their test. Eventually, the novelty of going in and out wears off and they become more amenable. This system also has the advantage that the horse's muscles do not get so tired. You can work a horse too long: the more tired he becomes the more his muscles ache and the more disillusioned and uncooperative he can become.

Similarly a horse can go 'over the top', that is become either so tired or so bored by the whole process that the test becomes listless and very hard work. If your horse has gone 'over the top', some-times a jump or even a short gallop can restore his spirits. I know of some horses who always go better having had a jump before their test. For them jumping is a release and having got it out of their system they then settle more quickly and are more responsive.

Many horses are better on a second day at a venue. With these individuals you always have the extra expense of going the night before so that you can work them on the competition site. The only consolation is that you also get the chance to walk the cross-country the day before – and risk having a sleepless night.

Whatever system you use and however long it takes, there is always the moment just before the test. This is when I pick up the reins, do a few transitions, shoulder-ins and lengthening and shortening to build up a bit of impulsion ready to go into the arena.

Maybe you are lucky and your horse needs only 15–30 minutes 'warming up' before his dressage. If you are, make the most of it, because where the event horse is concerned you are on the exception to the rule.

The Test

The time you are given to ride around the arena before your test is all too short. Therefore you need to be mentally relaxed and on the ball while the horse before you is doing his test. There is nothing worse than being late, still having your tack check to come and your boots removed, when you could be in there. So get all the preliminaries out of the way in plenty of time. Then, as soon as the rider in front of you has saluted at the end of his test, you can be in there starting to settle your horse.

I have always had to make a conscious effort to stay relaxed, to take the odd deep breath and let go of myself when first going into the ring. It is very, very important to be totally in control of yourself because the reins are amazingly good conductors of tension.

Inevitably, when you first ride around the arena the horse will be a little tense. Initially, therefore, I often start off in rising trot in circles and serpentines around the markers. Then, as the horse starts to relax, I go into sitting trot and shoulder-in. As the relaxation comes so you can start to think of the test itself, of doing some of the early movements to put them into the horse's mind – in particular his best movement. This is partly because the horse can do it easily in his state of semi-relaxation and partly to impress the judges. If you can really impress them just before you go in, they will be thinking in terms of sevens and eights when you come to do your halt, rather than fives and sixes. Cheating is not allowed – gamesmanship is.

Enter the arena off whichever rein the horse is straightest and always come on to the centre line at a tangent off a circle. If you over- or undershoot the centre line, you will never get straight and will end up progressing to X in a series of 'S' bends. I always try to show good movement outside the arena to impress the judges but once I am inside and on the centre line I start to throttle back and set up for a halt as it is very difficult for the judges to see how extravagant the movement is as you go straight towards them.

If you are lucky and the horse is really relaxed, you can 'go for it' and show your best at all the movements. Unfortunately that does not happen too often and because of bits of tension the rider has to be conservative in how much he asks of the horse. The whole test should be smooth and flowing and therefore you need to confine yourself to working within the limitations of your horse on any particular day. It is better to get a six or seven with the comment 'not quite enough' than a three or four with 'broke' or 'irregular'.

Showmanship earns marks, so try to show as much aplomb as possible and look as though you are enjoying yourself. If nothing else, be accurate because just by making your figures a good shape and by doing your transitions on the markers you can accumulate a respectable score, even when the horse will not relax and show off what you know he is capable of.

Be conscious of where the judges are and what they can see. You can make a far greater adjustment in the corners at H and M and even more at F and K, when you have your back to the judges, than you can coming the other way.

Things will go wrong but try to pretend that is what you meant to do anyway and perhaps the judge will not notice. On any account it is certainly not worth getting upset and drawing the judges' attention to it. Whatever has happened has happened and you need to be thinking about and preparing for the next movement, otherwise you will spoil that one as

well; if things are not going well, never ever allow the judges to see your discontentment.

Common Faults
The following common faults can normally be avoided if the rider is really concentrating:

Not establishing the halt prior to the rein-back.

Stepping back in the halt because the rider is using too much hand and the legs are not kept on.

Pushing out the hindquarters in the shoulder-in rather than bringing the shoulders in off the track.

Not setting up well enough for the half-pass, resulting in insufficient bend and quarters trailing.

Hurried lengthened strides, with the horse going quicker rather than lengthening; usually caused by the rider letting go the reins and not asking for the necessary engagement of the hindquarters to give the horse the capacity to lengthen.

Hauling the horse into a halt rather than preparing for it and asking with the legs and seat.

Falling around the corners instead of keeping the horse relatively straight and going round the inside leg.

Giving insufficient rein in the free-rein walk for the horse to stretch forward and down.

Not preparing for the canter strike-off, so that the horse comes above the bit or runs into the canter.

Inaccurate figures.

Inaccurate transitions.

THE JUMPING PHASE

Walking the Course
Having found the start and then the first fence, the first thing to do is to decide how you are going to get to it. It always helps if you can canter down the arena and past anything you think the horse may spook at so that he is as familiar as he can be with his surroundings before he starts jumping. Normally I then try to do a transition and a change of leg to get the horse to pay as much attention to me as possible.

If there is a left-hand turn to the second fence, I would plan to come to the first on the left leg, provided there was a nice smooth route through from that direction. I then walk the route I plan to ride, picturing in my mind what I am going to do with the horse on every turn and at every fence.

I walk the turns not too tightly and not too wide, being conscious of the whereabouts of the collecting ring, the horseboxes and any other distractions. I step the distances in the doubles and combinations and all the related distances, that is up to 20 yards. Anything over 20 yards really gives you time to set up and start again, so the distance is not so critical.

I try to picture in my mind how a combination or a related distance will ride. The type of fence at either end makes a big difference, particularly if a triple bar is involved, where you can take off much closer to the base than over an upright. Obviously a related-distance upright to upright will ride very differently from the same distance oxer to oxer.

At the end of the course, having checked on the location of the finish and decided exactly what I am going to do at every fence and down every line, I turn my back on the fences and go through the course fence by fence in my mind so that every fence and every turn is memorized.

Watching

Try to watch a few competitors to see how the course is riding, whether the distances are working out as planned or if there is an unexpectedly difficult fence. Check how tight the time is and whether others are finishing their rounds well within the allowance. If they are close to or even over it, then you may need to change your plan and turn a little sharper into or after fences. I prefer to save time in this way than by speeding up because it is more difficult to keep the horse balanced when he is going faster, and therefore the chances of hitting a fence are greater.

Warming up

Warming up should be as similar as possible to your jumping preparations at home. The aim is to make the horse supple, lengthen and shorten his stride and turn within the same rhythm and balance. Use the same type of fences as at home. For example, start over a cross-pole at the trot if this is your normal pro-cedure. Increase the size of the obstacle and practise over an upright and a spread.

I have always believed in not trying to help the horse too much at the practice fence, always drop-ping my hands, allowing the horse to use himself or make a mistake if he wants to and always putting him to a deep spot, in just the same way that I would at

home. Then when I go into the ring and protect him more by holding him off a fence and giving more support with the hand, I find I am that much more effective.

If a horse persists in playing football with the prac-tice fence, a good remedy can be to put two poles very close together in either the vertical or horizontal plane. It gives the horse that much more to look at, is quite legal and can dramatically improve the jump.

Only jump as many fences as are necessary to get the horse jumping well. This may be as few as four or as many as fourteen. As soon as he is going in good style, stop so that he does not become tired. If it is still some time before his turn, walk him about and then give him another jump over a decent upright just before going into the arena.

If the horse knocks a fence down while he is warm-ing up, do not become anxious or irritated, but keep putting him in deep and give him plenty of rein so that he can use himself. It is important that he should be learning from his mistakes and looking at the fence as opposed to thinking about you.

Riding the Course

Whenever you enter the ring you have to be ready to react to the horse's behaviour. Whatever the plan may be about saluting the judges and cantering down and around the arena to get the horse acclimatized, the most important thing is that you need him as settled in as good a rhythm as possible by the time you go through the start. Therefore do not be in a hurry. Do not be frightened to do another transition or another circle past a spooky jump in order to get the horse that much more settled before you start. You have a minute from the time the bell goes. It is surprising how much you can achieve in sixty seconds if you stay calm.

In horse trials there is always pressure in the show jumping. At a one-day event a fence down usually means that you will be out of the prize money. In a three-day event the same often applies but in this case you are on a tired horse and it is the culmination of six months work. The greater the pressure the more I tell myself to do the simple things – keep the leg on, the arm relaxed, the horse balanced and wait for the stride to come – over and over through my mind to stop the tension of the occasion affecting my riding.

Often plans go wrong and the horse starts to jump a bit quick. Do not be frightened to stop and start again, always being mindful of the time. Similar action may be required if the horse starts to become strong. Whatever happens, though, do not let the horse go underpowered, and keep your concentration right to the very, very end. I once lost a CCI in Munich with a fall at the last fence in the show jumping.

THE CROSS-COUNTRY PHASE

Walking the Course

The main object of walking the course is to plan the shortest and safest route round for you on your particular horse. To do this needs concentration, which is not easy if you go round with a bunch of friends and their dogs. Your final walk round should always be on your own so that you can concentrate all the way and memorize every move.

The Start Box

Make a note of how to get to the start box, how you can get into it and where there is to walk around before the starter says go. See how big it is and decide how long before the off you are going to be in there. I even think about which side of the box I need to come out of. A placid horse will often stand quite happily during the countdown whereas with a high-spirited horse it is often better to go in at the last moment, particularly if the box is not very big.

The First Fence

I am never in too much of a hurry going to this fence. The important thing is to get started, keep the horse on his feet and pop over it. Then I think of starting to settle the horse into the rhythm for the rest of the course.

The Line

I have always believed that the line taken is one of the keys to successful cross-country riding. To start with, for every 10 yards you cut off, you save a second or have another second to spend at one of the more difficult fences – depending on how you look at it. When I see people snaking their way between fences I often wonder if they realize how much time they are wasting. I wonder at the thought process when I see someone coming to a straightforward fence with a left turn after it and they jump it on the right and do not make the turn until three strides after the fence. It is amazing how much time you can save simply by going the shortest distance between the fences, by being economical with your turns before and after them and, where possible, by jumping the fences on the inside track.

I would, however, always compromise on the shortest route in the interests of good footing. There is no point going straight through boggy, stony or rough ground for the sake of saving a second. Your horse's legs are far more important. Similarly, horses do not gallop well on the sides of hills and it is difficult to keep your rhythm when the camber is all wrong. These are all factors to be considered when planning the best routes between the fences.

Again, at the fences themselves, the 'straight' route is not necessarily the quickest one if it means that you have to come off line to get to it or, alternatively, that you could leave your horse travelling in a rhythm by going a little further.

Another trick is to keep looking back at the previous fence or at where you have just come from to check that you are still on the shortest line. It is often easier to see when looking back whether or not you have been on an unnecessary loop between fences and on which side you should have jumped the previous fence.

The bigger the fences the more crucial the line into them. You need to be able to come exactly where planned, not 6in to the left or 1ft to the right. I often walk the last 50 yards to a fence six or eight times so that I know exactly where I am going to balance the horse up, where I am going to turn and which daisy I am going to ride over. At the fence I always line up the point I want to jump with something on the skyline so as to be sure of being able to see both reference points at the moment of truth.

A horse unattended but equipped for the cross-country phase!

I would also compromise over the shortest line at the bigger and more technical fences. The bigger the fence, the more accurate you have to be and the longer you need to be on the line on which you want to jump the fence. Similarly, horses always jump better towards daylight and when they can see a way out and where they are going.

The Approach

Cross-country fences are jumped in the same way as show jumps except that they are taken a little faster. Remember that cross-country is not about big stand-offs and galloping flat out at fences. It is about balance and rhythm, and keeping coming to the fences so that a consistent type of approach is developed, which helps the rider to get the horse to the point of take-off. The better balanced the horse and the more rhythm he has on the approach, the easier it

will be for him to jump the fence. If he is on his fore-hand or going too fast, he will jump flat and will have to stand off the obstacle to clear it. At many fences this can be dangerous.

The cowboys stand off one fence then get very close to the next. They might be successful at the smaller horse trials, but not when the fences become bigger and more difficult. That is why it is the same people who tend to be successful at the major events. Their technique is correct at each fence; their approach is consistent; the horse knows what to expect and this helps him to cope with what he is asked to do, especially in difficult conditions.

Some of the more difficult fences need a slower approach to give the horse time to look at them before jumping. At these more technical fences a greater safety factor must be built in. Therefore the horse must be in a balance and going forward at the

right speed and rhythm well before the problem fence, so that he has every chance, particularly at the more technical fences. If the rider has to make alterations to the speed and balance in the last few strides, it can be disastrous. Right or wrong, in the last few strides before a difficult fence the rider must be determined to go and if he is wrong he must just hope that the consequences are not too painful.

Balance

The degree of balance required varies from fence to fence. The more slope there is to the fence the less the degree of balance required. When jumping across country the aim is to go as fast as possible and one of the differences between a good and an average rider is the ability to balance their horse at speed. The bottom line is, though, that at every fence you have to slow down to the speed at which you can have sufficient balance to jump it safely. To jump a fence without sufficient balance is just plain dangerous. Obviously, though, you need less balance for a triple bar than you do coming downhill to a gate or coffin, therefore you can jump your triple bar much quicker than your gate or coffin.

When walking the course you need to plan where you are going to start to set up for every fence. Depending on the fence and the horse it could be 5 yards or 500 yards before take-off – it does not matter provided you have the balance required for lift-off.

Once a rider starts to think about jumping cross-country fences in this way, many of the horrors of riding fast across the country start to melt away. Big fences are not a problem for there is only one way to jump them – keep coming, keep balanced, keep hold and wait for the fence to come to you. Ensuring that the horse's head is up and keeping him balanced are more critical than in show jumping. Whenever you are in trouble on the cross-country, the age-old saying, keep hold and keep kicking, rings true.

How fast a fence can be approached depends largely on the balance of the horse. However, it is not only his degree of balance that must be taken into account but also how his balance is likely to be affected by the going. It is more difficult to balance a horse over deep, soft or undulating ground, for example, and allowance must be made for this. Going uphill is easy but along the side of or down a hill is more difficult and more time must be allowed

to balance the horse in front of the fence. If the fence is on the flat, the balancing of the horse can be left until later than when going downhill.

On every course there are four or five fences where time is not the major consideration. The coffin, sunken road, water, quarry, light into dark and certain line and combination fences would all come into that category. Here the criterion is simply to be on the right line going at the right speed with enough power and balance to jump the fence when you get there. It does not matter how long it takes to achieve it, as long as you have the essential ingredient when you come to the point of take-off. When planning your line of attack on these fences, remember that you always need to start your preparations slightly earlier than you think, just in case the horse does not come to hand as quickly as you had hoped.

RIDING THE COURSE: BASIC TECHNIQUES

As long as the rider can keep his horse on his feet, keep hold of the reins and keep the balance, the only variants into a fence are the pace and the impulsion.

If you are unsure whether a horse will, say, bounce or put in a stride, then always plan on riding for the more forward option but keep hold of the horse's head so that he can still put a shuffle in if he wants to. If you ride for the more cautious option, you often end up with a stop – or worse if the horse is feeling brave.

Picturing the Course

After each fence, and at the end of walking the entire course, I picture how I plan to jump each individual fence. I also check in the programme that I have not missed out a fence. Yes, I have missed fences both in the show jumping and across the country in years gone by. Then, just before getting on my horse for the cross-country, I go through the course in my mind again.

After walking the course my plan is so detailed that I know which side of each tree stump or cow pat I am going to go. I know to within 6in my track for the entire course. Often it will not work out exactly according to plan, so there has to be flexibility, especially on the younger horses. But even at the Olympic Games I would study alternatives at all the fences. Then whenever I am in trouble I can always switch to Plan B.

At the end of the day the most important principle in cross-country riding is to want to do it, to be committed, before you set off, to getting to the other side of every fence every time. Whether you are right or wrong, make the horse go. Never give up trying to jump a fence until the horse comes to a halt. Never accept a fall until the horse has actually rolled over. Always keep trying. If you are not certain about whether you want to go or not, do yourself and your horse a favour – don't start.

10

COMPETING IN A THREE-DAY EVENT

THE BRIEFING

This briefing, which normally takes place in the morning of the day of the first horse inspection, is when competitors are given details of all the arrangements for the event.

If competitors have not already had details from the stable manager's officer about stabling, feed, bedding, water and the muck heap, these could be given out at the briefing. They will also be informed where the vet and blacksmith can be found on the various days, what accommodation and meals are being provided and what has to be paid for, as well as the procedure regarding tickets and passes.

The organisers hand out a map showing the layout of the competition sites and the roads and tracks, steeplechase and cross-country courses. Competitors are told when and where they may or may not ride, drive and gallop; at what time and where they can jump the practice show jumps and cross-country fences; any special regulations regarding the various phases; and in particular how certain fences are going to be judged.

WALKING THE COURSES

The Roads and Tracks

On my first drive round the roads and tracks I try to assimilate the general picture of the route and I particularly look out for the good, bad and indifferent going. I try to memorize where the kilometre markers are, putting them on to my map for future reference.

If I am riding at a competition for the first time or the roads and tracks have been changed from previous years, I always try to drive round a second time when there are fewer people about and it is easier to concentrate. Some events allow people to ride around before cross-country day. This is something I have never done but I can see that it may be helpful to some riders and it is certainly useful where the hacking facilities are very limited.

Before I start on cross-country day I need to be absolutely clear in my mind as to the location of the compulsory flags, the kilometre markers and the sections of good footing, where I can make up time and the poor going, where I may lose time.

The Steeplechase

When walking the steeplechase I pay particular attention to walking any lines to or away from the fences and around the turns. I need to find out, or to measure myself, where the quarter, half and three-quarter distance points are on the course.

If the course consists of two identical circuits, walking it once is sufficient, but if it is a figure of eight or there are any loops then it needs more careful inspection. In this case its entire length should be walked at least once until you can clearly visualize the whole course.

When riding late in the draw, I have also always found it useful to go and watch a few of the early competitors on the steeplechase to see how the fences and turns are riding and to see how tight the time is.

The Cross-Country

Walking the cross-country thoroughly is critically important to a successful campaign at a three-day event. I always walk the course a minimum of three times. On the first inspection I simply look at all the fences and their alternatives and get a feel for the ground and the course as a whole.

The second walk-round is the time to start coming to some decisions. You know what the footing is like and what is still to come and you certainly need to decide on all the alternatives you know you can do. If you are still uncertain about any fences, I would go back and look at them again individually later in the day.

The third walk-round is very important. By now I have decided what I am going to do and this time I am going to ride the course in my head. It is therefore important to go by yourself and when there are not too many people around. I walk my exact line between every fence, ensuring that I am not travelling further than I have to, exactly where I plan to make my turns and set the horse up for every fence and to the inch where I plan to jump every obstacle.

Having completed my final walk-round, I always then go through it again in my head, perhaps when I am in bed, or on the loo on the morning of the competition, or in the stables: just somewhere where I shall not be disturbed and can play the whole action through in my mind.

WORKING OUT THE TIMING FOR PHASES A, B AND C

There are many ways of doing this. Some people simply work from a start and finish time, but I note down the time when I should be at each kilometre marker. I put the times on to two pieces of card, placing one in each pocket in case I lose one. The times for Phase A are in one column and those for Phase C in another; the card is folded to separate the columns (see diagram 00).

I put down the time at which I should be at the start of A then, working on the basis of four minutes per kilometre, at the first, second, third and fourth kilometres and at the finish of A, followed by the start of B and the finish of B. The start of B should be two minutes after the finish of A and the finish of B is based on the optimum time for the steeplechase.

In the second column, under Phase C, I allow six minutes for the first kilometre and four minutes for each remaining kilometre. I plan on finishing two minutes before the time when I would start incurring penalties. This gives me a little bit more time in the box and a little leeway if I start to get behind on the clock or if the last kilometre takes longer than planned because of people or traffic.

A		C	
Start A	13.25	1	13.54
	1 13.29	2	13.58
	2 13.33	3	14.02
	3 13.37	4	14.06
	4 13.41	5	14.10
Finish	13.42	6	14.14
		7	14.18
Start B	13.44	8	14.22
		Finish C 14.24	←Time I plan to finish
Say the steeplechase is 4 minutes 30 seconds – 13.48-30		Limit 14.26	
Allow 6 minutes for first km of C – 13.54-30		The limit is the time after which I start incurring penalties.	
Round the time down in case of finishing B earlier than planned. Then Phase C km one at 13.54.			

RIDING-IN

The riding-in starts with walking the horse out on the day of arrival, usually the Tuesday afternoon. I always show the horse as much of the site as possible at this time, allowing him to pick some grass to help him relax.

On the Wednesday I ride early, because the briefing is often at 10 a.m. If it is a horse's normal routine to be lunged at competitions, I would also put him on the lunge at a three-day event before riding him. At this stage, while riding I do no dressage but simply get the horse to trot around on a long rein. Normally he will be a bit tense so the major aim is to get him to let go. The length of time for which he is lunged and/or ridden depends on how quickly relaxation is achieved. With some horses it helps if they are taken for a hack. I often get my groom to take the horse for a ride after I have finished working him and while I am at the briefing.

With most horses, if I had a Thursday dressage, I would take them out again after the horse inspection. Again, though, I would be concentrating just on getting the horse to relax so that I could walk, trot and canter on a loose rein. The three-day event horse is so very fit and feeling so exuberant that this is often easier said than done. Eventually, however, following half-halt after half-halt, even the most effervescent horse will give in and become rideable.

I have to confess that I have been known to do a few movements at the end of this riding-in period, once the horse has relaxed. I am sure that the horse does not actually forget the aid for a half-pass, but somehow having reminded him I seem to sleep a little better. The great thing to remember is just to concentrate on what you know you can do and not try to improve on what you have been doing at home simply because, for instance, you have seen someone else do a smart extended trot.

FIRST HORSE INSPECTION

Your horse should be plaited up for the first horse inspection, which normally takes place during the afternoon before the first day of dressage. It is important that he is well turned out and that you make him look as smart as possible. It is the first time the judges will see the horse and there is some truth in the old adage that 'bullshit baffles brains'!

These days trotting a horse up is becoming something of a science. Ground juries are tolerating less and less in the way of unevenness, stiffness or funny action. Therefore you need to have rehearsed the best pace for your horse to trot up, the best position for him to carry his head, the best way of attaching the lead rein and the best position for you to run, in order to create as good a picture as possible.

Some horses trot up better after being ridden for twenty minutes or half an hour beforehand. If you are going to do this, be sure to allow enough time to dry off the saddle patch. A damp saddle patch conjurs up all sorts of nasty thoughts in the minds of a ground jury.

Be sure, too, to be smartly dressed yourself, as you are part of the overall impression: and be sure to look cheerful when you meet the ground jury.

THURSDAY

If my dressage is on the Thursday, I get that out of the way first before worrying about anything else. I have never been good, either mentally or physically, at coming back from a big course walk to try to ride a test.

Because the atmosphere is so different from that at home or at a one-day event, considerable thought needs to be given to how best to get the horse relaxed and rideable in the arena. The process may take three or four hours of having him in and out of the stable, lunged, ridden, lunged, ridden and so on.

If he is relaxed in one place, go for a hack, come back and pick up the reins in another. I have often tended to get my horses a fraction 'over the top' outside. I have found that the atmosphere in front of the grandstands always 'lifts' them when they go into the ring. However, I would not pick up the reins to do any movements until about 20 minutes before my test.

If I do not have a test on the Thursday, the day could consist of riding in as many times as necessary, combined with the cross-country course walk and a further look at the roads and tracks and steeplechase.

FRIDAY

If my dressage is on the Friday, then as on Thursday the day revolves around preparing for the test, before going for a final course walk. If the dressage was the day before, I might give the horse some light exercise before setting off on the roads and tracks, steeplechase and cross-country.

It is important to rehearse the trot up in order to create as good a picture as possible with your particular horse

I am not a believer in galloping after the dressage. There is seldom suitable ground for galloping and I have never been convinced of the merits of doing so. My horses would have had their last gallop on the Tuesday before travelling to the competition and if they need a little extra, there is always Phase A to warm them up.

WEIGHING OUT

At some events riders are allowed to weight out and put the saddle back on the horse in the stable. This is less unsettling than when it has to be done elsewhere. Usually, however, it has to be done at the start. Remember that on the one hand you must allow enough time for the weighing out and saddling up in the starting enclosure while on the other you must not let the horse stand around for too long or become cold.

TIME CHECK

Check that your watch corresponds to the official time before starting. This is best done before you get on your horse and again at the start of Phase A. I normally set out with two watches, a stop watch and my normal wrist watch as a back-up in case the stop watch gets stopped by accident.

PHASE A

Ride Phase A with your stirrups at the length required for the steeplechase. The important thing is to try and get the horse to relax. Ride on a long rein if possible and change diagonals every kilometer so that your weight is born equally on the horse's back. Where there is some good going the horse can have a little canter to warm up for the steeplechase. At the end of Phase A you should have two minutes spare before the start of B. This is the time to check your girths, tack and watch.

PHASE B

I use a stop watch for timing. I press mine to start when the steward says 'five' in his countdown from ten seconds to 'go'. I have always found it too difficult to start and press the watch at the moment the starter actually says 'go'.

On the first circuit I aim to be at the halfway stage at exactly half time. I should then have about five seconds to spare on the second circuit (because there is no standing start) so that if I keep going at the same speed I should come in five seconds early. If I am five seconds late at the halfway point, as long as I do not

Left: Weighing out
Right above: The rider making a time check at the start of Phase A
Right below: Phase A. The rider should change diagonals every kilometre so that her weight is born equally on both sides of the horse's back

go any slower I should be on time. But if I am more than five seconds down, then to be inside the time the horse will have to go faster over the fences and/or on the flat on the second circuit. I would only make him do this if I felt I could do so without tiring him excessively.

There should be no change in the approach to each fence. I try to keep the horse balanced on a nice holding stride and wait for the fences to come to me. There have been occasions when I have been behind on time after the first circuit and I have moved the horse to his fences a bit more, but I make sure that I put him back on his feet and just pop a fence or two before the last. Hurdling steeplechase fences can be a dangerous habit to get into just before Phase D, when you are going to require considerable control in order to jump 3 ft 11 in of fixed timber.

I check my watch at the quarter, half and three-

On the steeplechase the horse should be kept balanced on a nice holding stride and not allowed to hurdle the fences. Note the good position of the rider over the fence

quarter points because steeplechase penalties tend to be very expensive and I do not want to be late unless I have a good reason. Similarly, I never want to be more than five seconds early as that is a criminal waste of energy which the horse will need later in the day on the cross-country. You will also have put unnecessary strain on your horse's legs.

PHASE C

Remember that the clock is not stopped at the end of Phase B, so that if you finish a minute early you will start Phase C a minute early and will have to finish it a minute earlier than planned.

At the end of Phase B let the horse pull up in his own time, and as slowly as possible. Let him walk the rest of the first kilometre of Phase C so that in all it takes the six minutes allowed in your timing. While walking I let my leathers down three or four holes to save my legs before the cross-country. It is difficult to do rising trot with short stirrups.

Under FEI rules there is an official stopping place in this first kilometre where the groom can check the tack and shoes. The groom should take a spare iron, leather, bridle, girth and set of shoes in case of any loss or breakage on the steeplechase. There is normally a farrier there, who can if required replace any lost shoes. In a hot climate or when the conditions are humid the horse can be cooled by washing him down, sponging his mouth out with water and putting ice under his tail and over his head. Remember, though, that the clock is not stopped.

If the horse has had a hard steeplechase, for example because the going is soft or the conditions humid, I do not worry if I am a minute or two behind schedule at about the third kilometre marker of Phase C, as long as there is some good going on which I can canter later. It is important to allow as much recovery time as possible after the steeplechase and in those early kilometres of Phase C. Each kilometre cantered takes only two and a half minutes so it is easy to make up time. I am very wary about cantering on bad going, but the penalties are severe for being late – one penalty point for every second over, as opposed to 0.8 in the steeplechase and 0.4 in the cross-country.

When trotting I continue to change diagonals every kilometre.

THE BOX

Trot into the box on a loose rein so that the inspection panel can see if the horse is sound. This saves trotting him up again in hand. It is wise to stand up in the stirrups when doing this in case the horse is not even on both diagonals. Then stop and dismount and allow the vet to listen to the horse's heart and take the temperature of your horse. It is the vet's job to ensure that the horse is not lame or distressed, but I still check to make sure I am completely happy that there is no injury which could be aggravated by the cross-country and make it necessary to withdraw.

Ideally there should be a team of three to work on the horse in the box: one to hold him and two to work. I do not take the saddle off, because putting it back on is time-consuming; I just loosen the girths, run up the stirrups and loosen the noseband.

Tie stable rubbers above the horse's knees and just below his hocks before washing him off to prevent water running down into his bandages. Sponge him down with lukewarm water, or, in hot conditions, iced water, then use the sweat scraper to remove excess water and put a rug on him to make sure he does not get cold. Take the stable rubbers off his legs as soon as he has been sweat scraped. Check his studs and shoes and wash out his mouth with a clean sponge. A damp sponge can be used around his head and face. Get him walking as soon as possible to prevent him stiffening up.

The rider must keep warm, too, so put on a jacket. This is the most miserable part of an event. Ahead lies the most testing phase, and the nerves are in overdrive, not because of fear of hurting oneself but because of competition nerves.

Have a cold drink or at least wash your mouth out. Talk to people whose opinion you respect to confirm that your planned route is not leading to disaster. This is not the time to change plans unless earlier competitors have been getting into considerable trouble when taking your selected route. Check if other riders are finishing insider the time. Ask if the horses have been going very fast and whether they are looking very tired at the finish. If there seems to be a bogey fence, try to talk to people who have jumped it. But remember that your horse may be very different from theirs. Only listen to advice if the person concerned knows you and your horse.

After the horse has been walked for about five minutes you can grease his legs. This is supposed to help him to slide over any fence which he hits. I find udder cream the best because it is easier to remove but am sceptical as to whether or not it actually does any good. I believe it is a mistake to put too much on, particularly in a hot climate. Put a thin layer on his forearms, knees, the front of his body, his second thigh and his bandages. Be very careful not to get any on the reins, stirrups irons or saddle.

Make sure that your stirrups are the right length. I ride the cross-country one hole longer than the steeplechase. Then send the horse for another walk. Tighten the noseband, then another walk. Tighten the girth, then another walk. Get on when there are about two minutes to go and check your girths.

It is your responsibility to be at the start when the starter says 'go', and he will say it regardless of whether the competitor is there or not. It is best,

therefore, to have an assistant keeping an eye on the time.

PHASE D

I do not use time markers on the cross-country but try to go as fast as I safely can, taking into account how far there is still to go and what fences remain to be jumped. Many people, though, find it helpful to check their time against minute-markers around the course. These are not marked on the ground and have to be measured out and memorized.

The important factor is to settle the horse into a rhythm which suits the going, the conditions, the fit-

Greasing a horse's legs helps him to slide over any fence in case of contact. Around the boots this can be beneficial. It is often overdone though – how high up his legs does the rider expect the horse to hit a fence!

ness of the horse and the pace that can be maintained until the finish. This may have to be adjusted in bad going and when going up hills, and you will often have to give the horse a breather after a long climb. You can often speed up towards the end once there are only relatively straightforward fences left to jump. However, whatever your watch says, if the horse starts to tire halfway round, then slow down. You must ride according to what you feel underneath you rather than by your watch.

More and more competitors are becoming members of the 'watch brigade' and are basing their speed on it. Personally I have enough to think about without looking at my watch and am more concerned about how I feel the horse is going. There are occasions on fast ground and over simple courses when it is easy to do the time and then a watch is useful. But on more difficult courses it can be misleading because it does not take into account good and bad going, the different fences and what lies ahead.

There is a big difference between a one- and a three-day event. In the former it is possible to get away with going flat out from start to finish, but in the latter the pace has to be judged. Riding techniques which may not be essential in a one-day event become crucial in a three-day when the horse starts to tire towards the end of the course. He must be kept together and on his feet in front of the fences and given the necessary support from the hand. Learning to ride a tired horse is an essential skill. At the same time the welfare of your horse is your first and most important responsibility. At the end of the day this is a sport, not a matter of life and death. The welfare of your horse must never be put in jeopardy, no matter what your personal ambitions. Over the years there have been occasions when riders have been guilty of over-using their horses on the cross-country. They are regarded with disdain by their peers and public alike and never really recover from the smear on their reputation.

WEIGHING IN

Be sure to check the rules for weighing in. Do not dismount until you are told to do so by the steward and be sure to weigh in without a whip. Only the official steward can hold the horse and help you un-saddle, unless you've been told otherwise. The vets will want to look at the horse after you have weighed in but will not intervene unless drastic action is required.

SECOND HORSE INSPECTION

The second inspection takes place on the day of the show jumping phase. Once again it is important to have rehearsed for this so that you trot the horse at the speed at which he shows himself to his best advantage. This has become a very public occasion, when spectators can admire the heroes of the previous day at close quarters. I believe it looks bad to carry a whip. Once again, be sure the horse is well warmed up and that both you and he are well turned out and well prepared.

THE JUMPING PHASE

The warming-up takes longer than at one-day events because the horse will be tired and stiff after the cross-country. He will have to be loosened up and I find it best to use some shoulder-in, medium trot and 10m circles to make him more supple.

Normally I get on when there are fourteen more competitors to go, but I might do so even earlier if the practice area is a long way from the arena or if the horse is likely to be particularly stiff.

Running this phase in reverse order of merit puts more pressure on those riders who are well placed. It is important to make an effort to be positive in order to overcome the effects of the pressure of the occasion. If you become too cautious and think only about jumping a clear round, the tendency is to start hooking into the fences. This destroys the horse's rhythm, making him more likely to hit a fence.

Because the horse is likely to be tired and lethargic and will not be as sharp or have so much spring as usual, the rider must be sure to keep him going forward and balanced. Sometimes some extra pace is required on the third day to maintain the power. This is often the most searching test of a rider's technique, because now the horse is unable or does not feel inclined to come to the rescue as he might on a normal Saturday afternoon. It is on this third day that the hours of training put in over coloured poles can be so rewarding – or so heartbreaking if you as a competitor are found wanting.

11

CARE AT THE EVENT

Before you set off for an event an enormous amount of equipment has to be collected together and loaded into the horsebox. It is best to start by sitting down with a pen and paper and listing everything you need. If the horses are staying away overnight, the feed is loaded into the horsebox the day before travelling; the more valuable items are collected together in the tack room and then loaded first thing the next morning.

Remember, if you are travelling on the same day as the event, do not give the horse a haynet in the horsebox.

THE ONE-DAY EVENT

Dressage

The horse must be plaited for this phase. Plaiting is usually best done early on the morning of the test. If it is done the night before, the horse will probably rub the plaits and they will have to be redone.

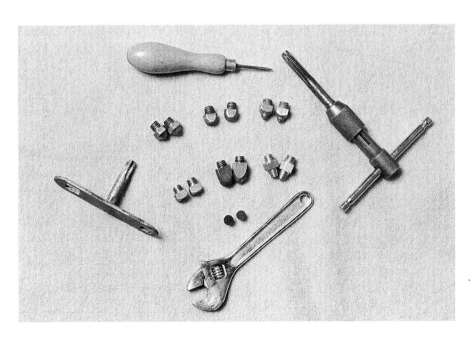

Studs and the tools for fitting them. The stud tap is used to check that the holes are clear before going to an event

Checking the tack trunk. It is best to start by listing everything you need before you start to pack

I put front and back studs in the horses' shoes on arrival and they are left in for the show jumping and the cross-country. The type of studs used depends on the state of the ground. Fine-pointed ones are required for hard ground, square-based with pointed ends for good ground and square ones on heavy going. Normally small studs are used in front and longer ones behind.

I use sheepskin numnahs, as they look smarter for the dressage, and often use a synthetic pad between the numnah and the saddle, particularly with the more 'backy' horses, to make it more comfortable for the horse to carry the rider.

In dressage the general impression is important so horse, rider and tack must all look smart. The rider's boots should be well polished and his coat and hat clean and shiny in the relevant places. Horses should be equally immaculate and I always think they look smarter with diamonds brushed on to their hind-quarters. There are a number of rules regarding the gear which can and cannot be worn. As they change from time to time, it is best to check in the current rule book. Having said that, I always work in for the dressage in brushing boots on the assumption that prevention is better than cure.

Show Jumping

If possible, I like to jump my horses in a snaffle bridle. Just occasionally, though, I have had to resort to other bits or a hackamore if that is what a horse goes best in. I prefer to jump without a running martingale but would always put one on if I thought there was a danger of the horse taking charge at any stage and running through his bridle.

Petal-type overreach boots. They can be fitted to each individual horse and do not turn up or break

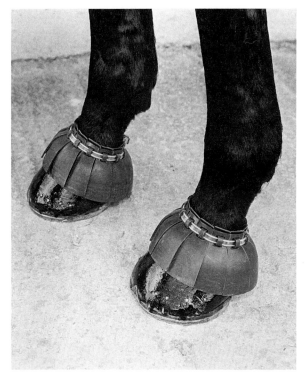

I only ever use a jumping saddle because I find general purpose saddles difficult to jump in. I also find the flat (American) saddles more difficult than the traditional English jumping saddle with knee rolls but this is very much a case of personal taste. It has to be said though that without the knee roll the position of the point of the saddle is much less relevant.

I normally put open-fronted brushing boots and overreach boots on for jumping. I find open-fronted boots the best for competition because if the horse is going to be careless, he might as well feel his mistake. As for overreach boots, I have found the ones with petals by far the best as you can make them exactly the right size for a particular horse and they do not turn up and seldom break.

Cross-country

I always undo the plaits for the cross-country but I leave the top one and tie the bridle headpiece back to it with a shoelace so that the bridle cannot come off in moments of stress. It is very difficult to catch a loose horse without a bridle and I have found a loose mane more sympathetic to my chin and easier to grab in those same heartstopping moments.

I use Vetrap bandages over Fibagee on all four legs. They have some stretch but do not slip. They should cover the leg from just below the knee to below the knuckle of the fetlock joint. The bandages are secured by sewing with criss-cross stitches, down one way and up the other. I do not use tapes, as they can come undone or, if the bandage slips, become too tight.

Bandaging must always be done with great care. It is very important that the join is on the side of the leg and not at the back of the tendon. I like to have a double thickness of Fibagee around the back of the tendon, making sure that the ends are on the side. To apply them, bandage for one turn at the top and then go down the same amount each turn so that there are equal amounts of overlap. Continue to below the knuckle and take the bandage up in the same way. The aim is to make the bandage firm enough to prevent any slipping but not so tight that it restricts circulation. It is a skilled operation and needs considerable experience. Anyone putting on bandages for the first time should seek help from a more experienced person.

For cross-country I use a bridle with rubber reins and whatever bit the horse goes best in. If it is needed, I put on a running or Irish martingale and I always fit a breastplate.

Studs should be worn on all but very sandy courses. More and more competitors now use two studs in each foot to prevent twisting, but I have not found that using one stud in each shoe causes more wear and am worried that the second stud on the inside could injure a horse.

A more important aspect of studs is choosing the right type for the conditions. Usually I keep to square-based pointed-end ones in front – it would have to be very wet before I used square studs in front. Some people do not use front studs at all because of the danger of a rider being trodden on, but I feel that by fitting studs you are much less likely to get into a situation that results in such an accident. On very hard going I sometimes just use road studs in front so as not to cause unnecessary jarring to the horse's legs.

Many riders wear spurs for the cross-country but I use them on very rare occasions. I feel that whenever one deliberately goes to use a spur the resultant loss of leg position and loss of balance does more harm than the spur does good. In fact, I think spurs should not be allowed across country because sometimes a rider can catch a horse by mistake in a stressful moment.

I wear racing boots because they are lighter and I have had a weight problem most of my life. Tights can be worn underneath to prevent rubbing of the knee and shin but I prefer 4in Elastoplast bandage covering the inside of the knee and shin bone. I use woollen gloves with rubber bubbles on the inside. These are less likely to slip than the more expensive leather versions. Mittens are also effective, but leather gloves become slippery when wet.

After the Cross-Country

After the cross-country the horse should be taken back to the lorry or stable. Remove the studs, pick out his feet and check for any sign of stones. Check, too, for cuts, overreaches or scratches, and if you find any remember to put on a poultice later, using Animalintex rather than kaolin on cuts or abrasions.

Wash the horse down, if possible with warm water, put on his sweat or thermal rug and walk him until he has dried off and stopped blowing. He can then be rugged up, given a small drink, preferably with the chill taken off, and bandaged. If he is to travel, put on his other gear and load him into the lorry.

I do not put kaolin poultices on a horse's legs following a one-day event because the next morning I like to see if we have done any damage. A poultice could possibly obscure a minor injury. If any problems do become apparent, the leg can then be treated accordingly.

When he gets back home or back to a stable the horse can be given a bran mash. If the weather is hot and he has sweated profusely, I put electrolytes in his water to prevent dehydration. During a hot summer I often use them all the time, not just after competitions. When electrolytes are given the horse should have two buckets, the second one containing plain water. It is important to give him the choice because he will only drink electrolytes when he needs them.

THE THREE-DAY EVENT

Many more preparations are needed for a three-day event than for a one- or two-day. It entails being away for five or six days; there is greater risk of injury or damage, so more spare tack is needed; and because the horse is at peak fitness and in strange surroundings he is likely to be more difficult to feed. He will usually need four feeds a day, with plenty of appetizers such as carrots and apples. The horse will need a passport if he is competing in a CCA or CCI.

I usually travel my horses to a three-day event on the Tuesday. As soon as they arrive they are unloaded then ridden about to see the sights. They can wander around the area of the dressage arenas and trade stands and pick some grass. They should be given plenty of time to acclimatize.

The equipment used in the dressage is similar to that for a one-day event, except that at all advanced events the rider should wear a top hat and tail coat.

In the stables try to keep to the routine used at home, feeding and grooming at the same time of day. On the Friday night before the cross-country give a normal feed but a smaller haynet. The haynet should be taken away six hours before the cross-country and if the horse is bedded on straw, he should be

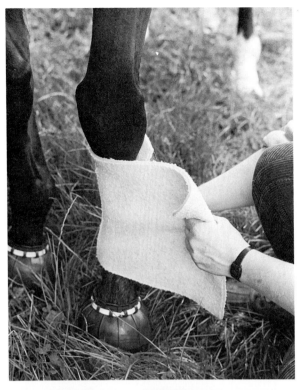

Fitting bandages is a skilled operation. A double thickness of Fibagee at the back of the leg, with the overlap at the side, protects the tendon. The bandage should be firm enough to prevent slipping but not so tight that it restricts circulation. Stitching is safer than a tape fastening for competitions

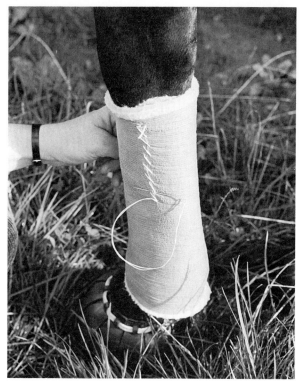

muzzled at the time of removing the haynets. A bowl of oats can be given as the breakfast feed unless the cross-country time is late in the day when a normal breakfast feed can be given. The last feed should be not less than six hours before starting the cross-country and water should be removed four hours before the off, except in conditions of extreme heat and humidity where the horse can be left with small amounts of water. Lead him out in the morning for a short walk at the time when he would normally be exercised at home.

Otherwise the horse should be given the same treatment as prior to competing in a one-day event.

After the Cross-Country

At some three-day events the horses can be washed off in the box but at others, such as Badminton, they have to be led back to the stables. Remove the bandages and all the tack other than the bridle before washing the horse down with warm water. The quicker this can be done the better. Remove the bridle if the horse is sensible, otherwise undo the noseband and throatlash and wash his head, mouth, between his hindlegs and down to his feet.

Get him walking as soon as possible and do not give him a drink until he has stopped blowing. Keep him walking until he stops blowing and is dry, then take him back to his stable. Put on another dry rug and keep him warm. Wash off his legs and take out the studs (this can be done earlier if there are enough helpers). Cold kaolin poultices on brown paper should be ready. Put them on all four legs, keeping them in place with bandages.

Once the horse has recovered he can be given a maximum of half a bucket of water which has had the chill taken off it. He can have a haynet and be brushed off. After this give him a mash, comprising one bowl of oats, two of bran, a little salt and his normal vitamin/mineral supplement, and obviously electrolytes if it is hot.

I usually trot the horse up to check for any unsoundness before putting him back in the stable and then again four to five hours after the finish, which will have given him time to stiffen up if he is going to. I take him out of the stable and trot him away immediately. If he has no problems, he is likely to be sound the next morning. If he is a little stiff, he is walked for twenty minutes and then trotted up again.

If he is lame, the cause must be found, so the bandages and kaolin must be taken off. Many injuries are treatable overnight. The Faradic machine is very good for muscle problems, the magnetopulse when there is some stiffness after a fall; and these days laser machines can also work wonders.

Legs can be given hot and cold treatment. I tend to use cold for the first forty-eight hours to stop bleeding and bruising. The use of hot before this encourages more internal bleeding. For a lump on the leg an ice pack seems most effective. If the problem is a bang or bruise, there is no reason why the horse should not be fit to jump. But if it is a strained tendon or ligament, then he will have to be withdrawn because jumping will aggravate the problem.

In trying to get the horse sound it is all too easy to give a forbidden substance. For example, some of the treatments used for overreaches at home contain prohibited substances, as does the Chloromycetin 'purple spray' and Dermoblian 'green ointment', so seek veterinary advice before applying or giving any medication.

To ease stiffness it may help to ride the horse out before the horse inspection. All my horses go for a half-hour walk beforehand to loosen up.

12

EQUIPMENT

In the stables I use New Zealand type rugs fitted with straps around the hindlegs and no surcingles. They do not shift and never give a horse sore withers. For a horse who is prone to getting cast I use an anti-cast roller over a pad and a Kiwi rug. The roller must be tight enough to prevent it slipping round.

Rugs made of materials which can 'breathe' are useful for drying off as horses do not 'break out' in them.

BANDAGES AND BOOTS

Most of my horses wear stable bandages when they are inside. For everyday exercise I use 'woof' type brushing boots or polo bandages on all four legs. However, I would not canter a horse in this type of bandage because it might slip. Overreach boots are always fitted when the horses are cantered or jumped and, as mentioned earlier, I find those with petals the most effective as they always fit well and never turn upside down.

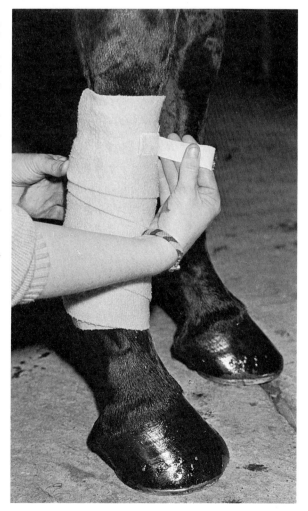

'Polo' bandages for exercise

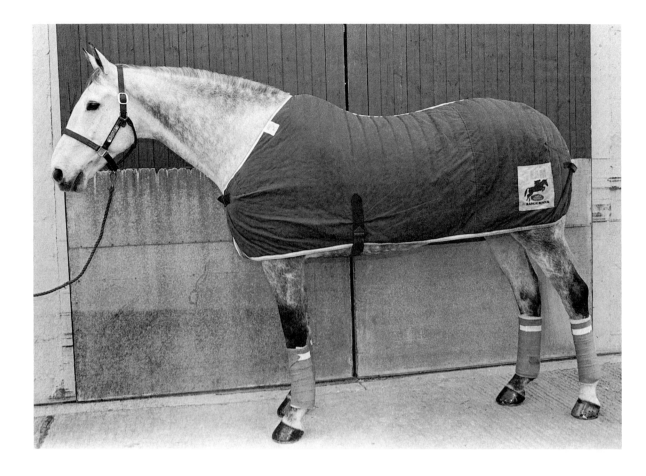

SADDLES

In the Pony Club a general purpose saddle is adequate but the serious competitor in adult competitions needs both a dressage and a jumping saddle. It is important that the saddle fits both horse and rider. It must be wide enough not to pinch the withers, but not so wide that it presses down on them. In dressage especially the larger the area of weight-bearing surface the more comfortable it will be for the horse. I have never been a believer in having a saddle with rolls behind the legs for dressage or jumping. The leg should not go back in the first place and, if it does, the rolls tend to ease the leg away from the horse's side.

NUMNAHS

I use cotton washable numnahs for everyday use, sheepskin ones for the dressage phase of an event and washable light cotton for the cross-country and jumping. As previously mentioned, most of my horses wear an orange or blue synthetic pad between the numnah and the saddle for added comfort.

Above: A horse wearing day run and stable bandages

Right: A horse fitted with a breastgirth, tendon boots and overreach boots: unattended but ready to go show jumping!

WEIGHT CLOTH

A minimum weight must be carried in advanced and international events and riders who are under 11st 11lb with their saddle must carry a weight cloth. For the very lightweight rider putting some of the lead in the saddle will help to prevent the weight cloth being too bulky and uncomfortable. Any weight which *is* carried in the cloth should be positioned with as much of it as possible as far forward as possible – preferably in front of the knee rolls. Never have any lead under the leg so that you cannot get your leg to the horse.

BITS

Most of my young horses are ridden in loose-ring Fulmer snaffles. As their training progresses I switch, wherever possible, to loose-ring German snaffles. If the horse is fidgety in his mouth, I try an eggbutt, but as soon as he settles I revert to the loose-ring German. These bits are much more malleable and give the rider much more feel. The type of loose-ring will vary from horse to horse, depending on the characteristics of his mouth. The lighter and softer

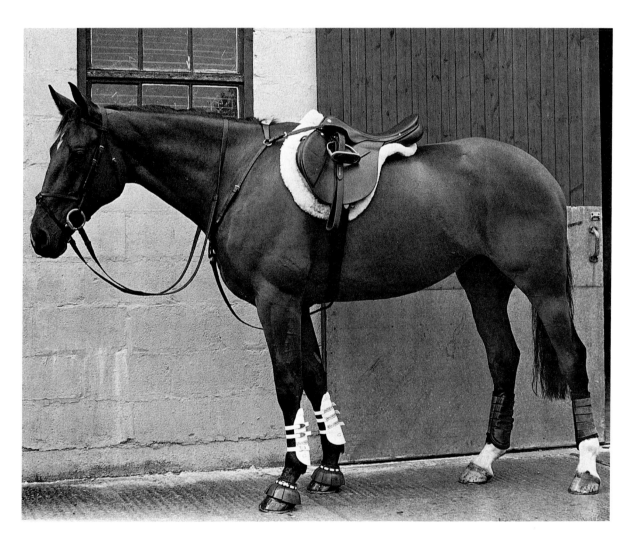

the horse the thicker the bit. The stronger the horse the thinner the bit and the more links you would think about using.

If the horse is heavy in the hand, try a light hollow bit. If this does not work, try a thinner or multi-linked mouthpiece. I frequently use a double-jointed bit but I do not like the Dr Bristol because the plate tends to damage the mouth and make the horse pull more as horses always run towards pain.

With a horse who curls up his tongue it is important to use the correct width of bit. If it is too wide, the centre will be low in the horse's mouth, making it easier for him to put his tongue over. A horse can get his tongue over a straight bar very easily but this type of bit is good for an individual who goes with his head in the air because it encourages a lower head carriage. The straight-bar vulcanite is particularly effective in this respect.

If a horse pulls, you have to ask yourself why he is being strong. Is he leaning, running through his bridle or simply wanting to go faster? Most horses get strong and pull because they are leaning. Sometimes a 'D' ring bit is enough to give the rider control but failing that I resort to a gag. Gags help to stop horses who tend to put their heads down, lean and pull. I have found the roller or rubber gags the most effective, but only use them as a last resort.

There are no hard and fast rules as to which bit to use. The important thing is to think about the action required, whether the horse puts his head up or down, pulls too hard or not enough. Make sure that the bit is not so severe that it hurts the horse – if it hurts, he will pull harder. Keep changing bits until you find the one in which the horse goes most kindly. Often a bit will work for only a short time. Many difficult mouthed horses need to have their bits changed frequently.

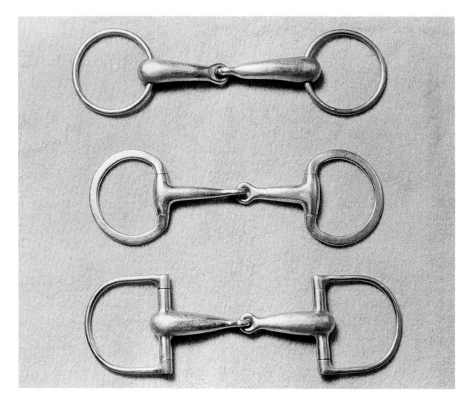

A selection of snaffle bits: loose ring jointed (top), eggbutt jointed (centre) and D ring jointed

A double jointed eggbutt snaffle (top), loose ring straight bar vulcanite snaffle (centre) and multi-linked Fulmer snaffle

A gag snaffle, useful on a horse who puts his head down, leans and pulls. The rubber gag, roller gag and American gag are all useful variations on the theme

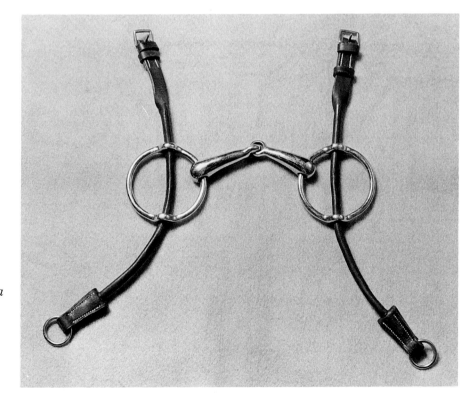

NOSEBANDS

Cavesson

The cavesson is the kindest and most widely used noseband. Cavessons come in different sizes and thicknesses but I like the thick padded ones, partly because they are softer and kinder to the horse, but also because they are the strongest and stretch the least.

Most event horses have to have their nosebands done up tightly to stop them opening their mouths at some stage during a dressage test. Certainly none of my horses have been sufficiently well schooled and soft enough that I could trust them not to show their teeth to the judges at some stage or other during a ten-minute test! To be fair, the event horse learns all sorts of bad tricks while he is out galloping on the cross-country course, which is why we so often have to use the noseband to help our cause in the dressage arena.

Flash

If the cavesson noseband alone fails to keep the horse's mouth shut, the addition of the 'flash' is very often the answer. Again it is important to do the cavesson up tightly in order to keep the jaw closed. The flash needs to be on firmly but not so tight that the horse cannot 'mouth' the bit.

Grakle or Cross

This is most effective with the horse who crosses his jaw. The cross-over must be either studded or stitched otherwise the action of the noseband is rendered useless. Again, the top strap needs to be done up tightly to stop the movement of the jaw and the bottom one firmly but not so tight as to prevent the horse mouthing the bit.

Drop

I am not an advocate of the drop noseband because it is very difficult to fit and does nothing that cannot be achieved by a flash noseband. Badly fitting drop nosebands cause more tension and therefore trouble in the mouth than they solve.

To fit correctly, the band across the front of the nose must be high enough to go over the part of the nostril that is all bone. It must not be done where the nostril starts to become fleshy on the side of the face. The band must also be short enough for the strap that goes under the chin to angle down comfortably under the bit without forcing it up in the horse's mouth. If the front band is too long, you can get the back strap under the bit only by letting the noseband down too low or having it fitting too loosely. Again it needs to be firmly done up but not so tight that it stops the horse mouthing the bit.

Correct Adjustment

Most people do their nosebands up too loosely. A loose noseband is there only for decoration and does nothing to assist the rider in getting the horse to accept the bit.

If you do your bottom strap up too tightly on a flash or Grakle, or your drop noseband is too tight, it can cause tension. But as a rule of thumb, if your horse is evading the bit or resisting the contact by opening his mouth, make life easier for yourself and do your noseband up tighter.

13

FEEDING

The secret of feeding is to feed according to the condition of the horse, the work required of him and his temperament. A shiny coat, loose skin and enough condition for the work he is doing are indications of good feeding. If the coat becomes dull and the skin tight, so that when a piece is pinched between the fingers it remains raised and does not return to normal for some time, and if the horse loses or gains weight, then check his diet carefully. If he is losing weight, make sure he is being given enough; if he is, then there must be another cause, which must be found and dealt with. For example, he could need worming or be suffering from a virus. If it is not a veterinary problem, consult a feed expert, who can analyse the feed being used and check that it is providing a balanced diet. In horse trials care must be taken that no forbidden substances are included. Therefore it is best to use proprietary brands which clearly state that they are suitable for competition horses.

Scientists are now proving what horsemen have, through experience, practised for a long time. Text books can only provide guides; the good horsemaster reacts to the way his horse looks and feels. The guide is that the horse's total daily intake should be 2.5 per cent of his body weight. The experienced person can estimate a horse's weight by looking at him, but special tape measures are available which give the approximate weight based on the measurement of the girth. The deeper the horse, the more he will weigh.

The intake of feed must be divided between bulk (hay, haylage, etc.) and concentrates of hard feed (oats, etc.). The ratio of hard feed to bulk can vary from 3:7 to 7:3. Getting the event horse fit entails gradually changing towards the latter ratio (70 per cent hard feed, 30 per cent bulk). The absolute minimum bulk intake is 0.5 per cent of the body weight. Changes to this ratio and any other changes to the feed should always be made gradually to avoid digestive problems. Horses are creatures of routine and are more likely to remain relaxed and therefore to eat up if their routine is maintained. Therefore I try always to keep to the same feed times even when the horses are travelling and away at shows.

The basic foodstuffs used in my stables are hay, bran, nuts, oats, micronized barley, sugar beet pulp and coarse mix. I give three feeds a day. The smallest one is given in the morning because the horses will usually be worked relatively soon after it (though not within one and a half hours of being fed). It is the feed which the horses are least eager to eat. It is always better to feed little and often rather than overface a horse with food.

THE VARIOUS FOODSTUFFS

Oats

Oats are the main energizer in my horses' feeds. The quality can vary enormously and the best test as to their value is whether or not the horses eat them. Sometimes my horses are reluctant to eat round shiny Australian oats but tuck into some smaller duller English ones and sometimes vice versa. The important point about oats is that they must not be dusty. I bruise rather than crush them as this makes them less dusty and is less likely to remove their goodness.

The amount of oats fed depends on the temperament of the horse and the work he is doing. I took one horse to Badminton on just 6lb of oats a day (though he was having extra cubes), but most horses at their peak fitness get 12lb. If the quantity of oats is reduced, then cubes, etc. must be substituted so that the horse still receives the same total poundage of hard feed. In the last month before a three-day event I give most horses as much as they will eat. Usually, if they are fed more than a certain amount they go off their feed. As soon as they do, cut back to the amount they ate up previously.

Young horses are fed much less because their high spirits must be kept under control: 6lb of oats is usually a maximum. If a horse has a difficult temperament, I reduce the oats and increase the nuts. Some horses become uncontrollable on oats, in which case I experiment, trying them on different types of cubes, everything from Racehorse to Horse and Pony.

Bran

Bran supplies bulk and protein, but very little energy. It is, however, difficult to obtain broad bran and today's varieties tend to be rather dusty. I feed bran twice a day and give bran mashes, to act as a laxative, after a competition and the night before a day off. The bran mash consists of one bowl of oats, two of bran, hot water and a handful of Epsom salts.

Cubes

I use cubes to give variety to the feed and as a means of supplying necessary minerals. A great deal of research has gone into compiling the leading brands and there is a good range of types for use in different circumstances. Horse and Pony cubes are non-heating and are not high energizers. I use them as the basic diet for young horses, horses just coming back into work and those who become scatty on oats. Because they are not supposed to supply enough of the feedstuffs needed for very hard work, most of my horses have their quantity of Horse and Pony cubes reduced and other foodstuffs substituted as they become fitter.

The other types of cube I use frequently are the event cubes, because they are guaranteed to be free of prohibited substances, and the Racehorse variety, formulated for horses in extra hard work. As the horses become fitter I substitute these for the Horse and Pony cubes. I find that many horses who become too high spirited on oats are easier to handle on a basic diet of Racehorse cubes.

Coarse Mix

Coarse mix can be used as a complete hard food but I find it too fattening and use it in small quantities in feeds as an appetizer. Most horses, even difficult feeders, find it very palatable.

Sugar Beet

Sugar beet is also a good appetizer but as it tends to make the droppings rather loose I tend to prefer coarse mix. Both are very fattening and so they should only be fed as an appetizer close to a horse trials.

Micronized Barley

Micronized barley is a high energizer and conditioner. I use it particularly in the early stages of getting horses fit to help build up condition and energy. It depends largely on the condition of the horse whether he is fed more or less barley or more or less oats. Thinner horses are given relatively more barley and fat ones relatively more oats, as long as their temperament can take the latter. As they get closer to peak fitness the amount of barley is reduced.

Micronized Maize

I have used micronized maize for horses who are very difficult to keep in condition, but it is heating and can produce little pimples on the horse's skin. It is also very fattening, so it is most useful for adding variety to the feed of horses who need to put on weight.

Barley

As with maize, if a horse is not eating up and is thin, I would try some boiled barley. It needs cooking for three to four hours and is often given the evening before a horse's day off.

Chaff

I feed a little chaff with each meal to prevent the horse from gulping his feed down too quickly.

Molassin Meal

Molassin meal is a good appetizer and I often use it close to competitions instead of sugar beet.

Salt

I put a sprinkling of table salt in each feed during the summer. It is particularly important if the horse is sweating a great deal, when he will be losing salt.

Electrolytes

In hot weather or when horses are sweating a lot I always offer electrolytes – always in a water bucket, never in the feed, and always with an alternative bucket of fresh water. Too many electrolytes in the feed can upset a horse's chemistry.

Supplements

I always use a vitamin and mineral supplement because it provides an additional insurance against loss of health. However, supplements are not so necessary if you are feeding 8lb or more of proprietary brands, which already have vitamins and minerals added.

Calcium

Calcium is the element in which horses are most often deficient, especially if they are fed a high-grain diet including a lot of bran, which leads to an imbalance in the calcium:phosphorus ratio. It can be corrected by adding limestone flour to the feed.

THE FEEDS

Most of my horses are large – 16.2hh and over – and for them a typical daily diet when they start work and are walking would be:

- 6–8lb oats
- 3-4lb micronised barley
- A handful of soaked sugar beet pulp twice a day
  or 2lb coarse mix in total
- 4-5lb Horse and Pony cubes
- ½ scoop of bran with the midday and evening feeds, but not in the morning

The above is divided in three feeds, the smallest one being given in the morning.

The amount of micronized barley, coarse mix and sugar beet fed will very much depend on the condition of the horse. If he is already fat off grass, there is no point in making him fatter and in such circumstances the quantities would be cut down to a handful only, just as an appetizer. If, on the other hand, the horse comes in looking poor, the quantities may be increased a little.

For a horse in fast work the following would be a typical daily diet:

a.m.	2 lb oats
noon	2-3lb oats, 1lb event cubes
p.m.	4lb oats, 1lb event cubes
later	2-3lb oats

Half a scoop of bran is given with every feed except in the morning and water is added where necessary. Evening feeds contain salt daily and supplements where required, particularly vitamin E and selenium. A handful of coarse mix, sugar beet or molassin meal is sometimes added as an appetizer if required. Electrolytes are given in warm weather and after competitions.

DIFFICULT FEEDERS

If a horse will not eat up, try giving him four feeds a day. Note at which feed he leaves most – usually it will be breakfast – and feed him less at that time and more at other feeds. Try appetizers such as apples, carrots and molasses, and old-fashioned remedies such as hanging up a little gorse in the stable. Picking at this often restores a horse's appetite.

BULK FEED

Hay

I like to feed a coarse hay with a good deal of timothy in it. More important, however, than its type is that the hay should be sweet smelling. If it smells at all dusty, I would avoid using it. My horses are given two nets a day, the first after exercise and the second at tea time. If they are in serious work, in most cases each net will weigh 8lb. It will be more when they first come in from the fields when they have less hard feed, and a little less as they reach peak fitness for a three-day event.

Horses who are prone to coughing are given hay

which has been damped with water from a hose. If this is not effective, the nets are soaked in a dustbin full of water; the morning net is soaked overnight and the evening one throughout the day.

Haylage

Haylage can be used if the soaked hay is not effective in stopping the coughing. It is a cross between hay and silage and is dust free.

WATER

Water should be freely available. The horse should never be fed until he has been offered water.

FEEDING AT AN EVENT

Horses eat up better when they can be kept to the routine they know, so try to feed at the same times as at home. For a one-day event no adjustments need be made unless the cross-country is around 9a.m., in which cases an early small breakfast will be needed. The only time when it is necessary to change the feed is before the cross-country in an advanced or three-day event. Then the hay is taken away six hours before the start and the water four hours before; only a small morning feed is given, consisting of a bowl of oats.

14

STABLE ROUTINE

The most crucial aspect of stable management is to stick to a routine and to be quick to notice any changes in a horse's look or behaviour. My grooms always inspect the feed mangers and the droppings to note if a horse has not eaten up or if the droppings have changed. The horses' legs are checked regularly and the girls know that there will be trouble if a lump or bump is not reported and I find it later. The legs must be cold and hard and it is vital to notice if anything anywhere is different from normal so that appropriate action can be taken at an early stage before any secondary problems set in.

EXERCISE AND GROOMING

My horses are fed at 7a.m. and riding starts between 8.30 and 9a.m.. Before riding, the horses are quartered so that there are no body stains, straw in the tail or debris in their feet.

For exercise I always use either brushing boots or polo bandages on all four legs. I prefer brushing boots to bandages because they seldom seem to cause a problem and are easily washed and looked after.

I use washable numnahs under the saddle and they are washed daily. I have had trouble in the past with horses sweating, being rubbed and getting sweat bumps, and this approach has prevented the problem. It is very important to keep everything clean. Another preventive measure is not to remove the saddle immediately the rider dismounts after a training session or competition when the horse has sweated.

Leave it for some minutes so that there is no sudden change of temperature or pressure on the horse's back.

During exercise, the rider on each horse I am not working myself that day reports to me if he has blown a lot, coughed, is lethargic or whether there are any changes in his attitude or way of going.

After riding, the horse's legs and feet are hosed if they are muddy. The saddle area is sponged down, as is the area under the girth and bridle. I have to be careful about mud fever in the spring, so the horses' legs (especially white ones) are dried extremely carefully. In the summer the girls hose down any horses who are warm, use the sweat scraper, fit a sweat sheet and walk them around until they are dry. Again they are checked for any signs of injury.

In the afternoon they are given a good grooming. I do not use machines but at the end of the normal grooming routine I do use a 'thumper', a leather pad, to tone up the muscles over the hindquarters and shoulders of the horse destined for three-day events. Hoof oil is put on the feet, and Cornucrescine if the feet are brittle.

TURNING OUT

If possible the horses are turned out for an hour a day. However, if this cannot be done regularly, my horses are not turned out to grass at all when they are in work. More injuries to fit horses are incurred in the field than anywhere else if they are not used to

147

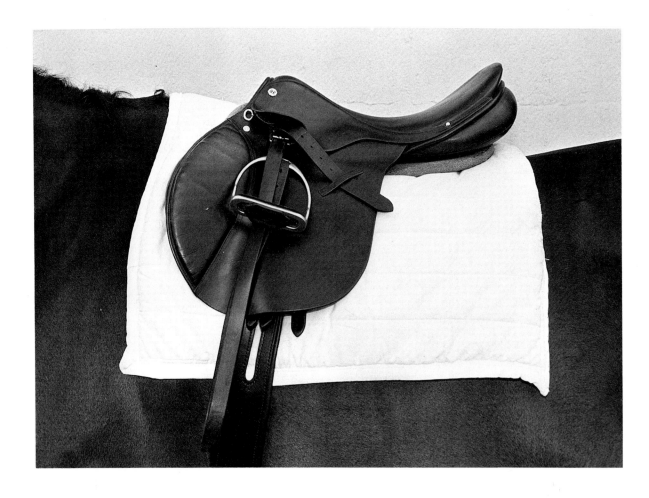

A jumping saddle fitted over a washable cotton numnah. The synthetic pad between the saddle and numnah gives the horse extra comfort. Note the forward point on the saddle. The lower the cantle and the flatter the seat, the better it is for the rider

the freedom. But they are led out to grass as often as possible, and always on their day off.

They go out to grass for their holiday, which usually starts after an event. This means that they have to be roughed off gradually. They are walked out for three or four days, depending on the weather, their rugs are removed progressively and care is taken to see that nothing sinister emerges from an injury or bang sustained at an event.

When they are first turned out a careful watch is kept on them for some time. If possible each one goes out with one other sedate horse. It is a great risk to turn horses out as a group. If necessary I get the vet to give the horse a tranquillizer on his first day out if he is very fit and has not been out for a long time.

SHOEING

The farrier is a very important person, for if he is good at his trade he can make an enormous contribution towards keeping horses sound. My horses are always hot shod not less than once a month, the frequency depending on whether the shoes are beginning to wear out, and whether there are any indications that the clenches are about to rise.

Because the horses will not be going to competitions when they come in from the fields, their first sets of shoes do not have stud holes. However, the shoes do have Mordax studs fitted to help prevent slipping during roadwork. It is only necessary to keep them in at later shoeings if the horse habitually slides a great deal or the roads are very slippery. As soon as competitions are planned, shoes with stud holes are necessary. The stud holes are kept clear of debris by being wedged with cotton wool. To make sure that there are no difficulties at an event, take the cotton wool out the day before, use a stud tap to check that the holes are clear and put in fresh cotton wool.

A shoe with stud holes. The holes should be kept clear of debris by being stuffed with cotton wool

If the blacksmith has done a good job, the shoes will fit, the nails will be level and the foot round. If the horse goes close behind, I like the shoes to be feathered. Problems such as going close behind or in front, when the horse marks his bandages or boots, not moving straight or forging should be discussed with the farrier, who can often make corrections which will help.

If the horse is flat-footed or tends to get corns, I use wedge pads and if a horse is worked on flinty ground, it might be advisable to put leather pads under the shoes.

Horses being aimed at a three-day event are shod just before the competition. This places a great responsibility on the farrier as it is so easy to prick the foot and make the horse lame. Sometimes I use a shoe which is about half the weight of normal ones – not a racing plate because studs have to be worn, but a lighter gauge metal. This set will be barely worn and can be re-used for future three-day events.

Normally as soon as the horse gets home from an event he is on holiday. He goes out in the field and usually has all his shoes removed. This does depend, however, on the ground and the state of his feet. If the fields are hard and/or stony, the front shoes at least are left on. It is important to prevent the horse from becoming footsore.

When a horse has foot problems the farrier can often help to alleviate or cure them with surgical shoeing. In such cases it is best to work with a vet and to follow his advice.

15

MAINTENANCE OF HEALTH

Keeping event horses sound is a major problem. Because the nature of the sport is to test their endurance, they are particularly liable to injury. There are, however, many preventive measures which can be taken to help reduce the risk. For instance, I have become more and more conscious of where and when to work and compete my horses. I try only to ride on good going and if it is hard, or rough or wet, I tend either to put them in a lorry and take them to better conditions for training or, if I am at an event, even to withdraw.

THE FEET

As all my horses' feet are X-rayed before purchase I always start with good ones. It is too great a risk to do otherwise, for the wear and tear of training and competing, when a horse has to gallop over all types of ground, exposes any weakness.

Even if a horse has good feet it is a mistake to work on hard ground, whether in dressage, jumping or galloping. If the feet are subjected to jar, it is all too easy for problems to begin.

The farrier can do a great deal to prevent and even cure foot problems. It is vital that the foot is balanced so that when it is seen from the front both sides are the same length and when seen from the side there is a straight hoof/pastern line – that is, the toe is neither allowed to grow too long nor cut back too far. It is also important for the heels to be open and for the shoes not to pinch, something which could lead to contraction of the heels.

Although I use wedge pads on horses who easily bruise their feet or are susceptible to corns, I rarely use pads which cover the feet and then only for a week or two. If they are left on for a long time, it is difficult to keep the feet in good order.

The warning signs of impending foot problems are when the horse loses his movement and starts to take shuffly strides; when he is unlevel on a circle but sound on a straight line; and when he will not stand off at his fences, drops short on landing or even begins to stop. In any of these instances the foot should be pinched with farrier's pincers to see if there is a tender area. Removal of the shoe often makes it possible to see if there is any bruising or any sign of corns or gravel.

If there are no obvious causes, I call the farrier and, if he is not successful, the vet. If the vet cannot find the problem, then I ask for a nerve block to check whether the trouble really does lie in the foot. If the nerve block confirms that it does, the horse should be X-rayed. The vet can nerve block first the foot, the fetlock and below, and then the knee and below in an attempt to isolate the problem area. Nerve blocking has an inflammatory effect and the leg(s) subjected to it may swell.

JOINTS

Wear of the joints usually produces windgalls. If these are to the rear of the joint and behind the suspensory, I am not too worried although of course I would rather they were not there. If they are in front of the suspensory, more often than not there is trouble of a more serious nature brewing.

At the first sign of windgalls the horse is put in stable bandages over Gamgee when he stands in the stable. If there are no improvements, the Gamgee is soaked in witch hazel and following the last exercise before a day off I apply Amoricaine or Ice Tight, which is washed off before the horse is worked again. Amoricaine cannot be used more than three or four times a week because it tends to blister.

If the windgalls are in front of the suspensory ligament, every time the horse is galloped it is at risk and the windgalls are likely to get bigger. A horse with such a problem should wear Vetrap bandages over Fibagee for extra support and protection whenever he is jumped or galloped, in addition to the treatment in the stable.

TENDONS AND SUSPENSORIES

Injuries to tendons and suspensory ligaments are every event rider's nightmare. Before being tacked up all my horses have their tendons checked, the girls running their hands down the legs to see if there are any variations. Anybody who has event horses should be clear about how to feel the flexor and deep tendons and the suspensory ligament. If you are not certain how to do this and to distinguish between them, ask a vet to show you. Horses do hit themselves and it is usually a disaster for a horse who has some heat in his tendon to be taken for a gallop. If it had been noticed before and poulticed for a few days, it would probably have meant only two or three days off work; but after a gallop the holiday could be rather more extended.

It is important to be able to distinguish whether heat and swelling are only on the inside of the leg, in which case the damage is likely to be the result of a bang, or if they are on both sides of the leg, when the injury is more likely to be serious and to require veterinary attention. Whenever there is doubt, call the vet.

An injury to the suspensory ligament is the most difficult to feel because there is usually less heat and swelling. The best way is to compare one leg with the other and to make sure that there are no differences in the feel between them, but even then it can be difficult to detect in the early stages and veterinary advice is normally the best solution.

If you are convinced that the heat and swelling have been caused by a blow, then as long as it was noticed early enough it will be sufficient to apply cold treatment, using ice, hosing and a cooling lotion. I soak Gamgee in a solution made up from material provided by the vet, and then bandage this Gamgee on to the horse's legs. For the ice treatment I sometimes wrap crushed ice in tea towels and hold the pack on to the damaged area. Alternatively, crushed ice can be bandaged on with Gamgee between it and the leg, but generally I find that it is easiest to use a proprietary ice bandage/pack.

After 48 hours the internal bleeding should have stopped, so change from cold treatment to alternate hot and cold. This will help to move the debris by getting the vessels to dilate and contract. I apply kaolin (hot) twice or even three times a day and hose the leg for 20 minutes between poultices. When the swelling and heat have gone the horse is slowly brought back into work, but I keep a particularly keen eye on the problem leg for some time after an incident.

Whirlpools, or large boots with a pump to circulate the water, are more efficient than hosepipes. The Americans use these, with ice in the water to help increase the circulation. They are useful but expensive.

I try as much as possible to prevent a problem developing into anything more serious. As horses cannot speak, an injury may not be noticed when it first starts to give twinges and if it is not, then when the horse next jumps or gallops serious damage can be done.

If the injury is more than a bruise or blow, or if there is any uncertainty, call the vet. Depending on the nature of the injury, he can advise as to what type of treatment is best, and whether the laser, ultrasound, Magnetopulse or Faradic would be of value. For serious cases I have found that a split tendon operation reduced the length of rest needed. Because a three-day event horse has only three or four years at the top it is important to get him back into action as quickly as possible, but having said that, the best cure for any leg trouble is always rest and time. Modern methods can, though, help the natural healing process.

Any horse whose legs tend to fill should wear stable bandages overnight.

SPLINTS

To detect splints run a finger up the inside and rear of the cannon bone - it is rare for them to occur on the outside. Once you can feel them, press to see if they are tender. If they are, I use Movalot and, if this is not effective, then rest is the only answer. Splints are usually the result of a blow or working on hard ground. To prevent them, all my horses wear boots or bandages and I try to keep off hard ground.

LUMPS AND BUMPS

In the early stages cold treatment is best for lumps and bumps because it helps to reduce the size of the leaking blood vessels. Forty-eight hours after the time of the injury, the analgesic effect of hot and cold may be used. In most cases it is best not to use heat, ultrasound, Magnetopulse or Faradic treatment for 48 hours after the injury is sustained so that time can be allowed for the natural healing process to block off the leaking vessels. Ultrasound can be useful if the swelling is the result of a bruise but it can cause damage, so either get a professional to treat the horse or ask a vet or physiotherapist to show you how to do it.

THE BACK

If I am concerned about a horse's back I call in a back specialist. I use a Faradic machine to help

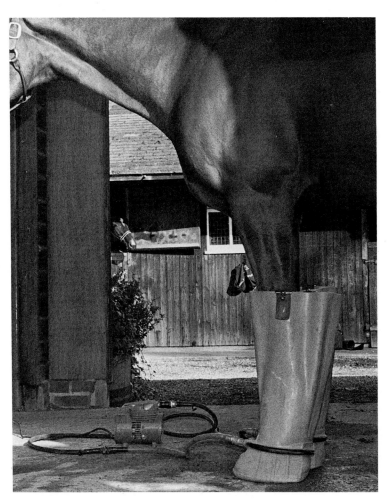

Whirlpool boots are expensive but more efficient than a hosepipe

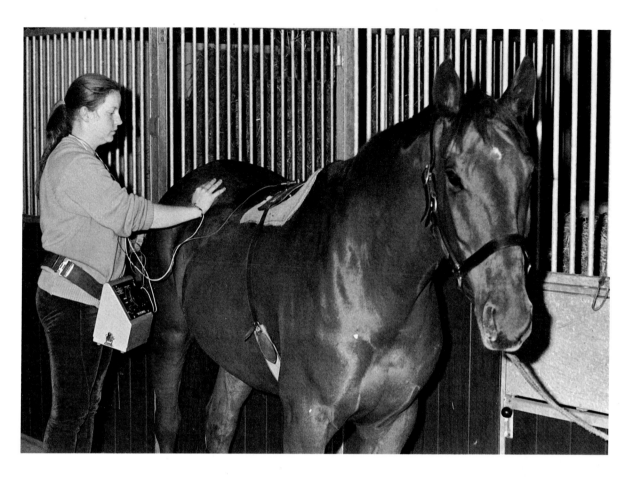

alleviate muscle problems which are often found around the back area. Cartier had a wasted hindquarter from an injury and was given Faradic treatment three or four times a week. The Faradic machine can also be used to detect where a horse's muscles are sore.

Another machine which is useful for back problems is the Magnetopulse. I have found that it helps to relieve stiffness as well as accelerating the healing of open wounds.

RECOGNIZING PROBLEMS

Often when a horse becomes stiff or resistant in his work, it is due to pain. Check for any signs of problems, particularly in his back.

In an effort to prevent pain in the mouth, my horses' teeth are looked at twice a year by a specialist horse dentist.

Faradic treatment is used to help alleviate muscle problems in the back and can be used to build up wasted muscle

WIND

When I first started riding in horse trials horses used to give the odd cough and caught an occasional cold; today the situation is much more serious. On our farm straw is abundant but fewer and fewer of my horses can be kept on it. As soon as a horse starts to cough I take him off straw and put him on to paper, dampen down all feeds and soak the hay. If this does not cure the problem, the vet is called in to check the horse's lungs with an endoscope. If that reveals a good deal of mucus, the horse is put into an environment which is as close as possible to being dust free. He is bedded on paper and fed on hay which has been soaked in water for 12 hours.

If the horse still continues to cough, then it is likely to be the result of a virus. I have used rhino-pneumonitis live vaccines in such cases and have found them effective so as a precaution I now give all my advanced horses this vaccine four times a year, in in addition to the normal flu vaccination.

Flu vaccinations are obligatory for competing horses, but I believe that they mask symptoms. This means that the first time one realizes the horse has a problem is when he is put under stress in a gallop or at a competition. Before the introduction of flu vaccinations, symptoms were more obvious and remedies could be given at an earlier stage.

BLOOD TESTS

I carry out routine blood tests to check that the horse has no infection or deficiency. The tests are taken when the horse comes in in January and again at the start of the season in March. I discuss the results of the January test with my vet to identify any irregularities or deficiencies and follow his advice on the correct remedy. I continue to test every three weeks until the blood profile becomes 'normal'.

The PCV count on the blood tests also gives an indication as to the fitness of the horse. This needs to be in the low 40s for the horse to be in a good condition to tackle a three-day event. If a record is kept of a horse's PCV counts, one fitness programme can be compared with another and used to check whether he is behind or ahead in his level of fitness for an event. In early March a horse who is going to Badminton should have a count of between 37 and 38, but by April it should be 41 to 42.

However, as each horse has a slightly different normal blood count it is his relative counts in different seasons which are most revealing.

WORMING

I have found that even after regular worming, and changes on to different brands, some horses still have a high worm count. Consequently I now stomach pump my horses once a year, which is not much more expensive and considerably more effective. This is carried out after their Christmas rest and if the worm count taken after it shows that they are clear, they are only wormed once more, after they come in from their summer rest.

I have used the above methods to try to keep my horses healthy and I selected them because I have found them effective through experience and not for scientific reasons.

16

TRAVELLING

EQUIPMENT

For a normal journey my horses wear stable bandages over Fibagee or travelling boots. Recently some very well designed travelling boots have come on to the market which seem to give all the necessary protection and yet are easily washed and maintained. The leg should be covered from just below the knee/ hock to the coronet. My horses also wear knee boots, a tail bandage and a tail guard. On a long journey I put Gamgee behind the straps on the knee boots. The number of rugs depends on the temperature and ventilation in different lorries and trailers. It is important to ensure that the horses are neither too hot nor too cold and they should be checked during the journey.

Hock boots are worn on long journeys, on aeroplanes and ferries and by bad travellers. The horse should be accustomed to wearing them, so remember to fit them in the stable at home on several occasions before he is actually required to travel. When horses are being flown I also fit a head guard to protect the poll. With some bad travellers, particularly on ferries and planes, I use overreach boots as well.

FEEDING

Horses should have their last feed at least an hour and a half before travelling. I only feed horses en route if they are making long journeys, in which case the feeds are mixed beforehand and given as near as possible to the horses' usual feed times. Before a long journey to the Continent the horses are given a bran mash the previous night and, if it is a very long trip, also for the three feeds the day before. Their feeds during the journey are also mashes. On most journeys the horses are given as much hay as they want.

ON THE JOURNEY

Horses should not be without water for more than four hours. Dehydration is one of the greatest risks of travelling and it is best to encourage horses to drink as much as possible. They should be given water at regular intervals on long journeys.

If they are going to spend many hours in a horsebox it is advisable to unload them occasionally and lead them out for a walk to stretch their legs.

Always try to keep horses at an even temperature when they are travelling. Adjust the rugs whenever necessary to prevent them getting cold or starting to sweat. On boats the temperature tends to vary dramatically and it is important that someone is with the horses to make regular checks so that the right type and number of rugs are worn to keep them warm but not hot.

LOADING

My horses are usually introduced to travelling by easy stages, as they start off by being taken to local

A horse dressed for travelling. If a horse is a bad traveller, overreach boots should be worn as well. Horses should be kept at an even temperature when travelling. Their rugs should be adjusted whenever necessary to prevent them becoming cold or starting to sweat

shows and going hunting. Before their first journey it is best to get them used to the horsebox and ensure that they load easily. It pays to be very patient in these early stages for if the horse is not frightened, and is perhaps fed in the box while it is stationary, and then on his first journeys driven very slowly, he is likely to be a good traveller for the rest of his life. Once a horse has been frightened it is very difficult to restore confidence and it might well limit his competition ability if he wastes a great deal of energy during the journey.

When loading do not try to pull the horse into the box or turn and look at him. Bullying a reluctant horse with a lunge whip is rarely successful. Instead try attaching a lunge line to one side of the lorry, take it around the back of the horse and have an assistant hold it. If the horse is particularly difficult and there are two assistants available, use two lines, the second attached to the opposite side of the box and again run around the back of the horse and held at the side.

Encouraging the horse to load by using two lunge lines. Both lines can then be pulled around the horse's quarters as the assistants move towards the lorry

The assistant(s) keep the line(s) tight while you lift the horse's feet one at a time and place them further forward. In this way little by little the horse is eased up the ramp into the lorry. He should be persuaded rather than forced to load. An alternative method which gives more leverage is to attach the lunge line as before, run it around the back of the horse, then pass it through a ring on the other side of the box and back to the assistant.

With a horse who is very difficult to load the important criterion is to put him in such a position that he cannot get away and cannot go anywhere else other than into the box. With such an individual I put the ramp down into the passageway running between the stables.

A difficult pony or small horse who does not kick can often by persuaded to load by two people standing on either side of his hindquarters and holding each other's wrists behind his quarters.

INDEX

Compiled by Gordon Robinson